Endorsements

"This book is something that I wish I had as I embarked on the path of collegiate athletics. This book has every tool necessary to successfully choose a college. It acts as a well-needed guide when opening the doors to a new and exciting chapter in a young adult's life. This is a must have for anyone that aspires to become a collegiate soccer player."

—*Kristin Ramaglia, Midfield,*
California State Polytechnic-Pomona

"This book is a great resource for anyone that's interested in playing any college sport. It gives helpful advice, loads of information, and a unique insight from college players themselves. Anyone looking to play any sport at a collegiate level should read this book! I wish that I could have had something like this to refer to during my recruiting process!"

—*Katie Behrens, Forward/Midfield,*
University of Tennessee-Martin

Pigtails to
PRESEASON

A GAME PLAN FOR PLAYING SOCCER FROM CLUB TO COLLEGE

Pigtails to PRESEASON

A GAME PLAN FOR PLAYING SOCCER FROM CLUB TO COLLEGE

GEORGIA L. HINMAN, Ph.D.
and soccer mom

TATE PUBLISHING & Enterprises

Published by Tate Publishing & Enterprises, LLC
127 E. Trade Center Terrace | Mustang, Oklahoma 73064 USA
1.888.361.9473 | www.tatepublishing.com

Tate Publishing is committed to excellence in the publishing industry. The company reflects the philosophy established by the founders, based on Psalm 68:11,
"The Lord gave the word and great was the company of those who published it."

Book design copyright © 2008 by Tate Publishing, LLC. All rights reserved.
Cover design by Jacob Crissup
Interior design by Benton Rudd

Published in the United States of America
ISBN: 978-1-60462-914-9
1. Sports: Soccer
2. Education: Higher
08.03.27

Dedication

Pigtails to Preseason is dedicated to all the female collegiate soccer players who responded to my survey. Thank you for taking the time to complete the survey; you truly overwhelmed me with your thoughtfulness, your insights, your advice, and sometimes, your very personal disclosures. *Pigtails to Preseason* is your story; I am deeply honored to have told it. My greatest hope is that I gave you the voice I promised. I wish you good fortune, happiness, and health as you embark on your next journey.

In Loving Memory

Kevin Houlihan, Kristin's first soccer co-coach and our family friend. He lived his life giving back to the soccer community. He was truly a great role model, a kind and gentle man, and a fair coach and referee. You will always be in our hearts.

Acknowledgments

To Kristin and Holly, my smart, beautiful, and talented daughters, *Pigtails to Preseason* is because of you! Through your soccer experiences, youth and collegiate, I gained knowledge and love for the sport, developed great friendships, and felt compelled to share with others what I learned. Thank you for all the soccer memories of driving to tournaments and camps, staying in less-than-reputable hotels, fighting with the airlines because your teammate lost her return trip ticket, spilling pop in the backseat of my minivan, weekly practices to Milwaukee, games in the torrential wind, rain, and snow, practicing in the backyard, meeting the Pelé look-alike and losing the bouncy ball collection at the USA Cup, playing nurse and doctor to girls who got injured or stung by a bee, and scrambling to find a jersey or a pair of shorts or cleats because someone forgot hers at home. Chaperoning teenage girls was like herding cats on a flatbed truck, and I wouldn't trade it for the world!

To Michael, my best friend and love of my life, your contribution to *Pigtails to Preseason* is immeasurable. You came up with part of the title, kept me organized, typed up all the player quotes, provided memories when I couldn't remember, and used your creativity to facilitate the book design. But most importantly, you gave me the encouragement, love, and steadfast support to write *Pigtails to Preseason*. Your unyielding belief in me was my inspiration.

To Kris, my traveling companion, roommate, and friend. I could always count on you for navigating through Chicago, spilling coffee down your white blouse, afternoon naps, shopping in Brookfield and arriving late to pick the girls up from practice, and great memories like your parents and the brush incident in San Diego.

To George, thank you for reviewing my initial cathartic rantings and for your sage insights and suggestions. You were always right! I couldn't have written *Pigtails* without your golden piece of advice: "Just an hour a day." It was my mantra.

To Sue Bee, thank you for your assistance with the data analysis and for being my editing queen. You don't miss a thing! I am grateful for your honest feedback that I'm "an okay writer and have promise," and for your wisdom and encouragement. Foremost, I thank you for your friendship.

To Angela Joy, thank you for giving me the words "your soccer experiences" to put in the subject of the e-mail to the players. It worked; they not only opened the e-mail, they responded!

To Jeff, thank you for bundling the e-mail addresses of the players by college/university.

To Kyle, thank you for coming up with part of the title and for marrying Kristin!

To Jane B, the person, thank you for being there to listen to my ideas, for your smart comments about my misuse of the English language, and for your friendship.

To Jane C, thank you for not allowing me my own pity party and giving me a deadline to identify and submit to one publisher by Friday. I found Tate the next day and submitted! How can a mere thank you be enough, my friend!

Table of Contents

Introduction

Since Title IX, the landmark legislation that created opportunities for female athletes, female participation in high school and college sports has increased significantly. A year prior to Title IX, in 1971–72, 294,000 girls played high school sports; contrast this with today, where nearly 3 million girls play high school sports. At the collegiate level, there were 30,000 female athletes in 1971–72; today there are 180,000 females participating in college sports.

Soccer is the largest growing sport and has been for the last twenty-seven years. In 1977, 2.8% of college campuses offered soccer programs for females; today, 89.4% of the college campuses across all three divisions offer soccer programs for females. Broken down by division, in Division I 90.2% of schools offer soccer programs, in Division II 79.5% of schools offer programs, and in Division III 95.2% of schools offer soccer programs for females.

Females represent 40% of college athletes and receive 45% of the $1 billion in athletic scholarships awarded every year. The opportunities for female soccer players to play at the collegiate level and receive an athletic scholarship are abundant and increasing.

Additionally, since Title IX, numerous research studies have reported significant long-term benefits for females who grow up participating in sports. Documented benefits include increased self-esteem and self-confidence, a better academic record in high school, an increased probability of completing college, a lower lifetime risk of developing breast cancer, and a decreased likelihood of depression, pregnancy in high school, and cigarette and drug use.

Julie Foudy, cocaptain of the U.S. women's team who won the Olympic Gold medal at the 1996 Olympics, says: "The thing I love about sports isn't just the thrill of winning, it's all the other things that come with it: the self-esteem, the ability to work within a group, to handle pressure situations, to overcome setbacks. You learn all these things on the soccer field."[a]

Brandy Chastain, two-time Olympic Gold medalist, says: "Football has given me everything. It has given me a place to express myself fully, openly, and honestly. To not be shy. To feel. To be crazy. To share laughter. To take risks. To try things I might not try. To make mistakes and realize they're not life-shattering."[b]

Pigtails to Preseason will teach players and parents how to tap into all the benefits—athletically, personally, and financially—that exist for young female athletes today. More than 1,600 female collegiate soccer players in Divisions I, II, and III were surveyed for this book. *Pigtails to Preseason* is a collection of their experiences. Through their answers to open-ended questions, players provide personal quotes, explain their decisions, and give advice to future collegiate soccer players.

Through the players' aggregate responses, the data identify important characteristics in a club coach, which gender is more demanding, and the life lessons they learned from their coach. Players share their experiences and advice about attending camps and tournaments for development and exposure to college coaches, the politics they experienced at the Olympic Development Program (ODP), and whether the sacrifices they made were worthwhile.

Players also explain what steps they took to get recruited, the number of club teams they participated in, the number of soccer camps they attended, how many created a résumé and/or videotape, and how many years they participated in ODP and at what level. Players also provide information on the types of activities they encountered on their official campus visits, how many received scholarship offers, and when an offer to play was extended. Players give information on the time commitment and intensity level for each collegiate division along with lifestyle, intensity, and commitment, broken down by preseason, in season, and spring season. Finally, players give advice on how to choose a soccer program and school.

Parents, you will learn how to guide your daughter by developing expertise in what to look for in club teams and coaches, which recruiting tournaments to attend and when, how to choose soccer camps, how ODP works and what to expect, when to create a résumé and videotape and what to highlight, what to expect when a college visit is requested, and how to help your daughter negotiate a scholarship.

Players, you will learn how to execute a step-by-step plan, both athletically and academically for each year of high school; to include which national tests you need to take; how and when to register in the NCAA's College Clearinghouse; and when to take your school's career inventory. You will also learn when to contact coaches and how to research programs, make a video, and create a résumé.

Through my Academic Questionnaire and Soccer Survey,

you will be able to articulate for which level of soccer you are best suited and establish and prioritize a list of required characteristics in a potential college. *Pigtails to Preseason* will teach you when, how, and what to communicate to college coaches and give you advice from current collegiate players on how to choose a collegiate soccer program and school.

Whether you are a player interested in playing collegiate soccer, the parent of a future collegiate athlete, or the parent of a child just starting her soccer career, your objective should always be to promote well-being, personal growth, and development along the soccer continuum. Given that players and parents may have differing perspectives on how to achieve these constructs, I have separated my comments, when appropriate, to parents and players within each chapter. You will find the following headings: "To the Future Collegiate Player," "To the Parent of a Future Collegiate Player," and "To the Parent of a Player Just Starting Her Soccer Career."

No matter what category you fall into, I encourage you to read each of the sections for a better understanding of your differing perspectives. And for the parent of a player just starting to play soccer, you will gain a longitudinal perspective that can facilitate you and your daughter's transitions through the soccer world. At the end of the book is a glossary of terms for novice parents and inquisitive younger players.

The Club Team

Finding One Is Like
Finding a Perfect Shoe

> Finding a club team is like finding a perfect shoe to wear—size, style, and durability. You want to make sure the players and coaches are the right fit, the team is flashy enough to be noticed by others, and the team and coaches will be able to make the journey with you and raise you to the next level of intensity.
>
> *Ashley Weimer, Defender,*
> *West Virginia University*

Introduction

Ashley's shoe analogy suggests an important construct—a good fit—between the players, coach, and the philosophy of the team. Finding this match is essential to the development, happiness, and self-esteem of a soccer player.

This chapter contains four sections: the first three address *the fit* a player must find with the team philosophy, her coaches, and teammates. The fourth section, player advice, is about finding the perfect club team. This section is all personal quotes from players to you, the player, about finding a club team that *fits* you and your long-term goals.

Data from players I surveyed is presented throughout each of the first three sections. You will learn the number of teams the collegiate athletes played for, why they left their club team, and their team's primary focus on winning, individual development, and/or team development. Players will also share their opinions on which gender is more demanding as a coach and how their club coach helped them in the recruiting process.

 To the Future Collegiate Player

If your goal is to play college soccer, you need to find a club team that is competitive and that attends tournaments where you can be seen by college coaches. Your club coach should focus on skill and tactical development, field positioning, both on and off the ball, and he or she should be able to communicate well and assist you in the recruiting process. The majority of your teammates should also want to play in college to ensure motivation to improve and commitment to the sport. All this will be explained throughout this chapter.

 To the Parent of a Future Collegiate Player

If you are a parent of a player, U–14 or above, who is considering a college soccer career, your job is about to get harder. As teams and players mature, their shared and individual goals may change. As your daughter becomes cognizant of her abilities and how they compare to her teammates' and competitors' abilities, she may need to seek out different experiences to further her development.

Her awareness of how she fits in the world of soccer may begin to shape her long-term goals of playing in college and the choices she will make to get there. Her growing ambition will compel you to redefine your role as her soccer experiences intensify. In addition to being your daughter's advocate, biggest fan, guardian of the house rules, and academic sentinel, you will now be her soccer broker. As her soccer broker, your new role will be to help your daughter sort out her soccer goals, locate appropriate experiences for her development, and encourage her, when she begins to evaluate her soccer expertise, to find the match between her soccer abilities, her academic goals, and a collegiate program.

To the Parent of a Player Just Starting Her Soccer Career

If you are the parent of a daughter who is just starting to play soccer, this chapter will teach you how to identify a team philosophy that is appropriate for her age, recognize good coaching in terms of their knowledge of physical and cognitive development of young children, and understand what should and should not be emphasized with this age group.

Your daughter's initial experiences in soccer will determine her future—whether she ever plays sports again, let alone soccer—and how she relates to people in authority, her perception of self as an athlete and a citizen, and even her health and academic achievement. A lot is riding on this early encounter!

Team Philosophy

On a younger team, focus should be on individual skill. The coach needs to be willing to work with individuals and keep an open mind about kids wanting to do other things besides soccer. At age eleven you will burn out if soccer is all you are allowed to do. Additionally, you have to have someone that understands the game and starts to teach the fundamental concepts of playing as a team. As you get older, I think knowledge of team and styles of play become much more important, as well as ability to train the players, developing agility and strength as well as a more complex understanding of how certain systems work.

Cassidy Acuff, Defense,
University of Texas–Dallas

To the Parent of a Player Just Starting Her Soccer Career

Team philosophy for the younger players is easy; it should always be about having fun! In fact, it is imperative at this developmental stage that your daughter experiences the sport in its purest form—for fun. With fun as the guiding principle, basic skills can be introduced along with the concept of "team." Each player's contributing role to the team's success should be highlighted and reinforced.

Success at this level should be defined within the context of happiness. Your daughter should be glad to go to practice and enjoy game days. Your daughter needs to feel valued for what she brings to the field. At this level, what she brings to the field is her positive attitude; her willingness to participate; her enthusiasm to try new things; her ability to focus, for at least a short amount of time; her feelings of happiness as she spends time with her friends; and her excitement for after-game treats!

This is where the foundation is created; this is where girls' soccer self-esteem develops and this is where dreams begin! In life we learn that sometimes just showing up is an essential ingredient to success; for your daughter, her motivation to show up provides the impetus for the dream of playing in college.

⚽ *To the Parent of a Future Collegiate Player*

Usually around U-14, club team coaches, players, and parents begin to rethink the team's level of play. If the team as a whole shows signs of potential, the coach may suggest moving to a more competitive division. If parents and players are happy, the team's trajectory may stay the same, and sometimes, if it's been a rough season, the team may opt to move down a division. If the latter two scenarios occur and your daughter has expressed an interest to play in college, she will have to find another more competitive team that will provide opportunities for continued development and knowledge of the game.

Whether your daughter moves to a different team or her current team advances to a higher division, everything is going to change. The scenario that follows is based on your daughter staying on her current team and the team advancing. If your daughter moves to another team, she will have to get to know her new team and coach in addition to all the changes I outline below.

First, the team philosophy may shift as decisions are made to become competitive. What was once a team focused on fun may switch its attention to competition and winning. Half-hour practices consisting of fun drills and scrimmages may turn into an hour and a half of focused practice. An outside trainer may be invited to teach speed or agility training, fitness, and/or nutrition. Tactical field play along with new and more challenging drills may require intense concentration and pressure during practice and daily practice and skills development at home.

Second, playing time in games may change along with tryouts for next year's team. With a focus on competition and winning, instead of all players playing an equal amount of time (which should always be the case for the younger teams), some players may begin to see very little playing time. Tryouts for next year's team may not include an invitation back for players who are unable to continue their development. These players will be replaced at tryouts with players who can augment the current team's composition and have the soccer aptitude for continued development.

Before these changes occur, it is important that everyone—the coach, the players, and the parents—all sit down together at a team meeting and discuss the implications of moving to the next level of competition. A sequential progression of a team looks like this: a recreation team may turn into a select or competitive team; a competitive team may turn into a regional traveling team. Within the competitive structure there are more levels, depending on your state. The ultimate level in the state of Wisconsin, for example, is the regional traveling team that forgoes the high school soccer season for the highest level of competition in its region. Teams may skip levels and age groups depending on their goals, soccer abilities, and competitiveness.

Third, there may also be an increased financial commitment with warm-ups, new bags, new uniforms each year, invited trainers and guest coaches, and expenses for out-of-town travel (i.e., gas, hotels, tournament fees, food, and frolic). Parents and players who do not agree with the direction of the team may opt out of the team at the end of the season.

When these types of decisions are being made at the team level, players are also internally making decisions on a very personal level about their soccer prowess, their commitment to soccer versus other sports and interests, and whether they want to go to the next level and eventually play soccer in college. This is where being your daughter's advocate is so important.

⚽ *To the Parent of a Future Collegiate Player*

The decision in front of you likely involves increased commitment of time and money to the sport of soccer, thus it may be time to sit down with your daughter and talk through the issues. As a parent, you must decide if this increased commitment is within the family budget and also within your own personal family philosophy. Is this what you and your daughter really want? Don't ever be afraid to find another team where the team philosophy better matches her/your vision.

⚽ *To the Future Collegiate Player*

As a player, you need to create a list of goals, short term and long term, and think through these questions: If you are a dual athlete, how will this new level of commitment affect your other sport? Do you have other interests or hobbies that require time? Are you willing to miss a high school dance and other events for soccer? How will this affect your ability to just be a regular kid? Do you have an interest in playing in college?

Make sure you have the same goals as the coach and you fit into her/his type of program. If you don't like your coach or her/his ideas, you will end up hating soccer and everything about it.

Anonymous,
University of Arkansas

Never feel guilty about leaving a team. You have to keep advancing and keep going to higher-level teams. No one will be angry at you for that; they will be cheering you on and hoping that you keep advancing.

Stephanie Barrett, Defense,
University of Massachusetts

Additionally, as teams evolve from recreation to competitive/select, the shift in the team's philosophy toward winning often goes unnoticed. Winning becomes synonymous with competitiveness.

If a team's philosophy is predominately about winning, then other things may become neglected. These may be things like player and skill development, self-esteem, and life lessons about commitment, motivation, and teamwork.

With a sole focus on winning, some players' contributions to the game may be minimized or they may be replaced by other players the coach believes can deliver the win. In this environment, players are valued in terms of their contribution to the win. (By the way, this is the philosophy of many collegiate programs, especially in Division I. It is not about individual player development, it is not about fairness, it is not about life lessons, it is about delivering the win at all costs. There is no such thing as equality at the collegiate level.)

But in club soccer, at all levels, it should be about player development, life lessons, and the contributions each player makes to the team. I'm not suggesting that all things should be equal, only that every player receives equal opportunities to develop and refine her skills, demonstrate tactical and strategic aptitude during games, and play a role in the team's wins and losses.

There are two things that distress more parents than anything else and are talked about at length along every sideline at a game: (1) the issue of playing time and (2) fairness. Problems unquestionably emerge on teams as treatment of each player is dependent on what their contribution is during a game.

For example, a player with natural abilities who scores goals in every game but doesn't attend practices may actually be allowed to start and play entire games over players who attend all practices but whose contribution during the game is viewed as minimal. With the focus on winning, the coach may not only play this player in games but give them a starting position! This may, in turn, cause team dissension, feelings of unfairness, changes in motivation and commitment levels, destruction of the team concept, and even a change in how the players feel toward this teammate.

Soccer is about more than winning. I believe a club coach who promotes winning over everything else is missing an opportunity to teach players life lessons that will enrich them personally and serve as a foundation for them in college and in their professional careers.

> A good club coach must be able to look past
> the winning aspect of the game and focus on
> the skill and technical development of the team.
> Many times my club coach would make us

do something during a game that would look completely ridiculous to an outsider but was an important aspect and effective way of teaching us a fundamental component of the game. You have your whole college career to focus on winning. Your high school and club years should be spent mastering the basics because this is what will get you on a collegiate team that wins games.

Anonymous,
Pennsylvania State University

A good coach is someone who understands the potential of each player. There are girls who may not be as good but have an enormous heart for the game. Don't deny them their chance to play just to get another goal.

Suzanne Smokevitch, Defense,
Michigan State University

A good club coach is one who realizes that we're paying outrageous money to improve and that getting time in games rather than winning is what is important to us. This is what creates a great atmosphere.

Laura Tuveson, Goalkeeper,
St. Michael's College

To find out what was emphasized on the collegiate players' club teams, I asked players, "What was your club team's focus: individual development, skill development, and/or winning?" The data indicates that winning was less important than individual and skill development with the exception of players who went on to DIII schools. I'm not sure why this is the case. I am encouraged that most players who went on to DI and DII teams had a primary focus on skill development and that DII players had club teams that put a minimal emphasis on winning.

Club Team Focus	DI	DII	DIII
Individual Development	74%	73%	58%
Skill Development	84%	84%	69%
Winning	71%	39%	71%

Coaching

A good coach is someone you want to sit by at dinner.

Anonymous,
Mesa State College

This quote is so simple, yet so powerful. I think it speaks to an entire constellation of variables essential to each player's development and future. It speaks of respect, trust, and integrity, which are foundational attributes to a person's character. It implies certain constructive behaviors and attitudes that become evident through personal interactions and contact at practices, games, and team events. This section teases out the important behaviors and attitudes essential for coaches along with their subcomponents; examples are provided through quotes from players.

When I asked players: "What characteristics make for a good club coach?" they articulated eight variables. Just as the player from Mesa State implied, they are all rooted in respect, trust, and integrity. The eight variables identified were: a good educator, respect, motivational, fun, understands gender differences, fair, playing experience, and is able to help with recruiting.

A Good Educator

> I've had the experience that teachers (high school) make the best coaches. They have the ability to teach the game and explain its most creative details.
>
> *Kimberly Weiss, Goalkeeper,*
> *California State Polytechnic–Pomona*

A good educator suggests more than just communication skills and, according to Kimberly's quote, along with the players who responded to my survey, this was the case. Players talked about how important it is to have a coach who can break down the game into tactical, technical, physical, and mental components. Even more important, the coach must be able to teach each of these components and subcomponents to all of their players, regardless of skill level or position on the field.

Moreover, a player's improvement depends on the coach's ability to communicate effectively and consistently through feedback. Players talked about the benefits of formal and informal evaluations. Informal evaluations are verbal and occur at practice and games. They are constructive and specific. Formal evaluations are written and may occur one to two times per season. They inform the players about progress over time and suggest adjustments to be made and skills to be refined.

A good coach is someone who will give me an honest opinion and tell me what I need to know and hear. Sometimes being a coach can be more than just a leader or an outspoken person; they create a positive environment for you to succeed.

Kaylin O'Shea, Midfield/Defense,
Western Kentucky University

It is very important that a player know her progress as she develops, so corrections can be made.

Amanda Garcia, Midfield,
Clemson University

A good coach always has something to tell you that you can do to make yourself better as a player.

Brittanie Waddell, Forward/Midfield,
Iowa State University

A good club coach must understand the complexities behind each player's personality and be able to motivate her in her own special way.

Ashley Weimer, Defense,
West Virginia University

Respect

Respect is a construct that can be conveyed by both words and behaviors. With words, there are the words themselves and the delivery, or the tone and the decibel level. Put together, they communicate respect or a lack thereof. The words themselves can be both positive and negative, and the tone can be soft, normal, or angry. Additionally, the decibel level can be low, normal, and loud. Respect is determined by each permutation or combination of these variables.

For example, if the coach's words are negative and their tone is angry and their decibel level is loud, this sends a pretty powerful message to the player, perhaps an unintentional message, nonetheless a message that lacks respect. Contrast this to the coach's words that are negative and their tone is soft and their decibel level is normal, this expresses a very different message, a message of respect and caring for a player's personal development. Thus, delivery is the key.

> Anyone who knows the game and the tactics can teach, but it is the heart of the coach, the passion they have for the game and team and their ability to gain the respect of their players that truly sets them apart from other coaches. It is how they deliver the message.
>
> *Anonymous,*
> *Michigan State University*

Behaviors are more concrete and easily identifiable as respectful or not. According to the players I surveyed, a coach who demonstrates respect exemplifies the following behaviors: instills discipline, is approachable, takes the role seriously, asks for input, knows each of the players personally, connects with the players, emphasizes team morale and not just winning, understands soccer isn't everyone's life, is a positive influence off the field, is committed to the team, is a role model, supports players, and is a professional. Now that is certainly a tall order to fill!

Motivation

What I learned from the players is that it is important to have a coach who is "motivational."

They talked about having a coach who motivates without degrading. Many players expressed concern with coaches who criticize their performance by attacking them as a person, not their play. Examples of this would be name calling, negative references to intellect, and creating a derogatory nickname (even in jest, it isn't funny to the recipient). Constructive criticism is an important part of development; it should only refer to the behavior exemplified on the field, nothing else.

There is also a difference among players regarding whether yelling is helpful or not. It appears to be very person-specific. Yelling will be addressed in the section on gender differences.

Overall, players want a coach who challenges them to try new things, asks them to dig deep inside themselves and give more, expects the very best from each player, is passionate about the players and the game, and can encourage them even when times are difficult.

⚽ *To All Parents*

From a parent's perspective, there are some questions you can continually be asking yourself as you watch the coach interact with your daughter, the team, and parents at practices and games. Words can be misleading, behaviors cannot. Here are some questions to get you started:

- Why is he or she coaching?
- Does she or he have goals for the team?
- Does he or she have something worthwhile to convey?

- What is his or her coaching philosophy?
- Is she or he a good role model?
- What life lessons do I want my daughter
  to learn?
- Is she or he someone I want to teach
  life lessons to my daughter?
- How does he or she give feedback?

I think the coach should be able to keep making the players better.

Jennifer Walters, Defense,
Auburn University

Fun

I learned from my club coach probably the most important lesson of all. At the end of the day, season, etc., soccer is still just a game. If we are not having fun anymore, it is okay to walk away. Soccer is a game, and a game should be fun.

Laura Crews, Forward,
Pfeiffer University

Soccer is *fun* and winning is not everything, just a bonus reflected from hard work and desire. When you walk off that field, you leave everything that just happened over the last ninety minutes there.

Erin Young, Defender,
University of Oklahoma

Most players believe that it is the coach's responsibility to make soccer fun. Players talked about the importance of wanting to go to practices and games because there is always an element of fun. A good coach promotes fun on and off the field and recognizes when players aren't having fun.

Fun is motivational. Fun is why players continue to play. Fun is an attitude and it's a behavior. As an attitude, it is lighthearted. Within a serious practice, there is the knowledge that at any moment it may give way to something spontaneous and fun. It is a positive energy that permeates words and actions; it is everywhere. It is the concept of "we," and it is inclusive of all.

As a behavior, fun can take many forms. It is a good laugh about something during practice or a round of World Cup at the end of practice or a team dinner after a game; players believe fun is fundamental to their soccer experiences.

> Find a club team where there is a good atmosphere and they can still take soccer seriously. You should always have fun with whatever you do; otherwise, it's not worth doing. If you can find a club team where they can have fun and still take care of business in a professional manner, then you found a good club team to be associated with.
>
> *Anonymous,*
> *Clemson University*

Imagine your thirteen-year-old daughter has spent the last two days at an intense tryout for a top competitive team. The coach of this team is an ex-collegiate female athlete who is young, pretty, and brimming with enthusiasm and expertise.

As a parent you realize you want your daughter with this coach. She is experienced, credentialed, knowledgeable, and appears to be here for all the right reasons. She has no children, just a husband. She merely wants to give back to her community.

As a little girl with a world of dreams not even realized and a bit awestruck by an ex-collegiate athlete, your daughter wants desperately to be a part of this team.

Two days after the tryouts, your daughter wakes up to find her house completely covered in toilet paper and a sign on her front lawn congratulating her on making the team. As a parent, you understand this is where you want your daughter. It is already fun.

Understands Gender Differences

I asked players two questions about gender differences in coaches: One, "Which gender is more demanding?" and two, "How would you characterize the differences in male and female coaching styles?" The first question is quantifiable, meaning I can present the data in a table, and the other is open-ended. The open-ended question provided the greatest breadth of information and also the most difficult to quantify. I have tried to tease out the themes players mentioned, but I think the quotes give us the best sense of what players believe is important for you to consider.

Let's start with the easiest: "Which gender is more demanding?" I categorized the data into responses based on divisions of soccer in order to maintain consistency throughout the book. I did not expect to find differences *between* divisions, and there were none. There were also no differences *within* divisions; they all believe male coaches are more demanding. The response of "unsure" was given by players who had only experienced one gender for club/high school soccer.

Gender Differences	DI	DII	DIII
Female	23%	34%	24%
Male	55%	50%	56%
Either, it depends	20%	11%	17%
Not sure	2%	5%	3%

I think it truly depends on the actual coach. Female coaches can relate more to a female team, to an extent. On the other hand, a male coach is an outside source with a driven purpose.

Jen Condon, Defense,
Mary Washington College

For the question "How would you characterize the differences in coaching styles?" players had different things to say about each gender.

For female coaches, I identified five categories from player quotes:

- Their ability to understand female players, meaning they are more sensitive, they usually don't yell, they are good listeners, and they know how to motivate.
- They focus on the mental part of the game.
- They focus on fitness and skill development.
- They know the game because they have played in college.

- They are more relationship-oriented, meaning they build relationships with players, they like to earn the respect of their players, but they can be moody and hold grudges.

For male coaches, I identified six categories from the player quotes:

- They do not understand females.
- They are more demanding, meaning they are scary, intimidating, and punishments are worse.
- They have poor communication.
- They are logical, which to the players means fair and honest.
- Their focus is on winning, not on relationships, they don't care if you like them, and they don't change their style to fit a player's mood.
- They are not always knowledgeable about the game.

I think the players' quotes say much more than I ever could to explain their perspectives.

> A good club coach has to know the difference between coaching guys and coaching girls. Girls require a little more patience and a little more encouragement.
>
> *Kathleen Blake, Goalkeeper,*
> *Catawba College*

It's like black and white; female coaches are more emotional and mental, where male coaches are all about winning and playing well. They don't seem to realize that there is so much more going on.

Kate Lowe, Forward,
East Carolina University

A good club coach must be tolerant of individual differences between players. They must also be demanding of each player as well as supportive. This is especially true with female players. Females all function differently. Some feed off of aggression while others need positive reinforcement constantly to get the best out of them. A good coach can recognize these differences and cater to the needs of his or her players.

Anonymous,
Stonehill College

I think a female coach is much more understanding than a male coach. A male coach is out there trying to understand what it is like to be a female athlete, while woman coaches know already and don't need to waste time.

Courtney Crandell, Forward,
Auburn University

Males don't understand the personal and day-to-day things that females go through that can impact mood and playing ability. Female coaches can understand where you are coming from. I think another huge difference is the way they actually coach. Men tend to yell and scream more, where women tend to be more demanding but do it in a way that motivates girls instead of making them hate them.

Erica Baker, Defense,
Western Kentucky University

Personally, I don't think there are differences between men and women coaches. I have had both men and women coaches. The majority were men and they wouldn't deal with the bickering and such that girls do. The women coaches, in my eyes, focus more on fitness. You have the ability to relate to them better.

McKenzie Burman, Goalkeeper,
Catawba College

I think male coaches are a little harsher. Some don't know how to coach girls. Girls need a little bit of sensitivity when it comes to certain things. When coaching guys, a male coach can yell at them for fifteen minutes straight during halftime and then the guys will go out and play that much harder to fix what they did wrong. For females, if this happens at halftime, most likely the second half is worse than the first because the girls are *too* concerned with what they are doing wrong rather than just playing the game.

Chelsea Hipley, Forward/Midfield,
California State Polytechnic-Pomona

I have found that both men and women can be equally demanding as coaches. Sometimes the men do not know how hard they can push their female players, so they are not as strict. Other times, the men drive their players into the ground. I have also had a female coach who worked us like crazy, the whole time making us yell, "We love fitness."

Elizabeth Pitti, Midfield,
Mary Washington College

A male coach is very direct. They do not sugarcoat things when you are not playing well, and they won't pat your back. They expect the most out of you physically and technically and want development on your own time. Female coaches have shared similar experiences and know about the game from a woman's perspective. They have higher demands in the area of tactical ability.

Amy Holst, Midfield,
Ball State University

I think when coaching females it is important to realize that girls bring everything from their day to practice each night. A good coach finds a way for girls to forget about all the drama and focus on what they love.

Jessica Parker, Forward,
Catawba College

Typically, males seem to be less approachable and less influenced by players and parents. In my experience, males seem to be more competitive and focused on winning. Females seem more emotional. However, a strength shared by many of the female coaches I have encountered is they are more open to new ideas, new drills, new strategies, and seem to always be looking to learn more about the game and about coaching. Females seem to be more reflective of their coaching, self-evaluative, wondering if they could have done something differently that would have changed the outcome.

Kristen Werder, Forward,
Clarion University of Pennsylvania

A male coach doesn't really want to know about the "girly" problems and just hopes you push it off and forget about it, whereas a female coach goes easier on you. Girls have the tendency to take yelling harder and female coaches know that.

Dana Stordahl, Midfield/Defense,
Southwest Minnesota State University

Fair

Fairness is a construct valued by most, but practiced by few. The saying "life is not fair" is something we learn to incorporate into our daily speech as the observance of fairness is left by the wayside. As kids, we are taught to be fair; as parents with children, we try to treat our children justly and teach them the merits of fairness and civility. But sometimes those life lessons are sublimated by people focused on opportunity.

Many players talked about a coach's drive for winning or their descent into politics at the expense of fairness to players. Players believe everyone should have to run at practice unless they are injured, everyone should have to attend practices to get playing time and especially to start the game, everyone who commits similar team infractions should be held to similar punishments, and players who work hard should be played over players for whom the coach feels sorry for or who have an influential parent.

These examples represent such a simple concept; I am continually amazed at the frequency with which I hear about them. Oh, and as a side note, this occurs at the collegiate level, too!

> A huge part of soccer at any level is politics. It is incredibly important for a coach to make his or her own decisions and not be influenced by parents.
>
> *Cori Shepler, Midfield,*
> *Clarion University of Pennsylvania*

> Find a club team that you can grow with. *Do not choose a club team based on politics!* I can't stress that point enough. I have seen so many problems with that. Politics ruin the game.
>
> *Kimberly Weiss, Goalkeeper,*
> *California State Polytechnic–Pomona*

Playing Experience

> A good club coach is a coach who has experience playing soccer. I feel that you gain the most knowledge with experience of the game. A coach can be very book smart about the game, but if he or she has never played at a high level, the coach won't know very much. It is easy to

learn the rules of the game; the hard part is being able to relate to the kids when you have never been in their shoes.

Nicole Munoz, Midfield/Defense,
California State Polytechnic-Pomona

Players believe an effective coach should have experience playing at a high level. They talked about being able to demonstrate skills, understand strategic play within all positions, and have the knowledge to prepare a player for college soccer. They said if the coach has played at the collegiate level, the players trust how far the coach is pushing them.

In analyzing player quotes, I found that players believe that more female coaches have played collegiate soccer than male coaches. As I thought about this, I started to count up all the club coaches my two daughters, Kristin and Holly, have had. Between the two of them they had fourteen coaches—five female and nine male. Out of the nine males, two played; out of the five females, all five played collegiate soccer. This is definitely something to keep in mind when reviewing coaches' credentials.

⚽ To the Parent of a Future Collegiate Player

I would encourage you to check into your daughter's coach's soccer credentials. Does she or he hold coaching licenses? Has she or he attended coaching clinics? How is her or his reputation in the soccer community?

Now, of course, when your daughter is U-8, parents end up coaching them, so I am talking about when they make the transition from recreational to competitive soccer. This is where you want to start looking for a coach with college experience and the appropriate licenses. And as your daughter makes that decision to play college soccer, a coach that is committed to helping her with this process is important.

My favorite coach was a female college player from Butler University. I was a junior in high school when she coached my club team. She possessed soccer skills herself and was able to play with us and to personally show us drills. We respected her because of her abilities. When she made us do conditioning, we had no complaints because she knew what was reasonable and the limit to which we could be pushed because she had done it before. She motivated us by understanding us and finding what made us tick.

Kathryn Austgen, Defense,
Colby College

You never find a woman coach who doesn't know her soccer, yet you find a lot of male coaches that don't know a lick of soccer and still become a coach, because males can get away with working only on fitness.

Kari McCullough,
East Carolina University

Female coaches are a little bit tougher because they know what it is like at a collegiate level, and they understand what it takes to be the best. Men's and women's soccer is so different, so I think female coaches have a leg-up in terms of understanding the girls on the team and knowing what level they can play at.

Tenesha Duncan, Forward,
University of Oklahoma

One would think that female coaches are more understanding, but from my own personal experience, I believe they are more demanding and less understanding. Many female coaches have played at the collegiate level and demand excellence. They push us to our limits and do not strive for that personal relationship that other coaches might look for with players.

Anonymous,
Canisius College

Recruiting

A good club coach has good contacts and a good reputation in the soccer community for recruiting.

Amy Holst, Midfield,
Ball State University

I asked players, "Did your club coach help you with the recruiting process? And if so, what did he or she do?" The first question was easily quantifiable and the data appear in the table below. As you can see, 55% to 75% of all club coaches helped their players in some way. There is a difference of 20% between DI and DIII players, for which I have no explanation. Reasons run the gamut; I just don't have the data to make even an educated guess. Let's just leave it as the majority of club coaches helped their players with the recruiting process. Yippee!

Club Coach Assistance	DI	DII	DIII
Helpful in Recruiting	75%	68%	55%

In response to the question: "What did your club coach do to help you in the recruiting process?" I categorized their responses into five categories, three of which are self-explanatory: explained the process, contacted coaches, and took players to showcase tournaments. The fourth category, hands-on help, and the fifth category, follow-through, are explained below.

Hands-on Help

Players talked about their coach helping them with their college application and their letter of interest to potential coaches, wrote letters of recommendation, and asked parents to create player profiles to be distributed to college coaches at showcase tournaments. This category impressed me the most as these coaches clearly went beyond what might typically be expected.

Follow-Through

Follow-through simply means many coaches were diligent in reminding players to keep up with the process of sending applications, writing letters, identifying programs, and motivating them. A phrase that I read over and over again was "kept on my case."

I believe club coaches have a certain level of responsibility in helping their players get recruited; however, it ultimately is the responsibility of the players and parents to make this happen, and it starts with choosing the right club team and coach.

I remember when my younger daughter, Holly, was overwhelmed and stressed with the recruiting process. Her high school coach said to her, "Good things happen to good people." Those six words carried Holly, her dad, and me through very tense times. It became our mantra. To Chris Martinelli, Edgewood High School's varsity girl's coach, thank you!

When I asked players, "What life lessons did you learn from your club coach?" I was awe-inspired by the effort the players put into responding to this question. Because their responses were so powerful, I think you might get more from just reading them than by me listing and explaining them.

However, as a person trained in gathering data, I did code their responses into five different categories: work ethic, integrity, professionalism, perseverance, and a positive mental attitude. The categories and examples are listed at the end of this section.

> My club coaches taught me a lot about life. They taught me how it's important to work hard and never give up on your dream no matter how hard it gets; that reaching your goals is never easy; and that you have to work really hard if you want to make it to a higher level.
> *Jessica Hussey, Goalkeeper,*
> *James Madison University*

You get out of life what you put into it.
Kaelyn Caldwell, Midfield/Defense,
University of Massachusetts

I learned many things about myself. On the soccer field, you encounter a wide variety of personalities and situations. Your character is shown both on and off of the field. I have learned how to treat teammates. I have found that you also have to stand up for yourself and know your physical limits. I have learned that respect for yourself and from your teammates is essential to success. I have learned what kind of person I am from playing soccer. Soccer has taught me about patience and perseverance.

Anonymous,
Canisuis College

Don't let people determine your future; you are in control and you have the ability to do whatever you want.

Anne Burnett, Defense,
Texas A&M University

This is actually funny because all through high school I hated my club coach, but looking back on it, I wouldn't have been able to play college soccer if it wasn't for him pushing me and training me as hard as he did. I think the biggest thing he taught me was to work hard and never give up. There were nights when I didn't want to train or run, but I wouldn't have been so successful if I hadn't done those things.

Erica Baker, Defense,
Western Kentucky University

I think my club coach taught me most about being good people.

Anonymous,
Lawrence University

The biggest life lesson that I learned from my club coach was to never give up on yourself and always be positive. I also learned to always play your game because someone is always watching you, and if you don't play the game that you know how to, you may blow your chances. Moreover, I learned not to be too hard on yourself when you mess up because everyone makes mistakes and those mistakes can be fixed; so don't be afraid to try new things, even if they don't work out the first time. But more importantly, I learned to go to the field and have fun, because only when you have fun do you play your best game.

Mallory Reid, Defense,
Mesa State College

Even though you may not necessarily be the biggest, fastest, strongest, or best player, you get out there and play like you are and you will be remembered by all those who cross your path.

Anonymous,
University of North Carolina-Pembroke

The only person who can really make a difference is you. Someone is always watching; they're not watching you to see how good of a player you are, but how good of a person you are. You must take the passion for the game and apply it to your own life and everything you do. You should never waste your time giving anything but your best. Be willing to adapt and anticipate. Life is important and you should never just wait for things to happen. You must make things happen.

Larissa Strychun, Forward,
Northern State University

Don't try to be better than anyone else, work to be better than you were yesterday.

Katheryn Kramer, Goalkeeper,
Winona State University

Practice makes *permanent,* because perfect does not exist!

Jodi Kulinitch, Forward,
University of South Carolina-Aiken

My club coach was diagnosed with cancer and through his battle with this disease he never let it get the best of him. This transferred right over to our soccer team. He taught us that even in the most adverse conditions, one must believe they can prevail and in turn they will. Before each game he would say to us, "There is no place I'd rather be than right here, right now. When it gets too tough for the other team, then it's just right for us."

Jess Conrad, Goalkeeper,
Lebanon Valley College

No regrets! Play each game as if it were your last. There were a lot of other lessons learned along the way, but in learning them, they become a part of daily life.

Jessica Jones, Forward/Midfield,
University of Wisconsin-Platteville

I learned to be gracious when I lost. I learned to multitask in order to balance school, work, and sports. I learned how to be a team player. I learned how to set a goal and work hard to achieve it.

Mary Elizabeth Fulco, Goalkeeper,
University of Mary Washington

Soccer is a big game consisting of all fifty-fifty balls/plays, so if you win the fifty-fifty balls/ plays, then you can win the overall game. This applies to life in that you should work to win the little battles, and if you do, then you can win the big war. Be proud of little accomplishments.

Anonymous,
University of Indianapolis

Most of life's lessons, I've gained through club/high school soccer. Determination, letting things go, my work ethic, respect, working with people you don't like, and responsibility.

Gina Chiello, Midfield/Defense,
University of West Florida

My club coach taught me a lot about how to deal with the mental aspects of the game and overcoming confidence issues. My coach also taught me not to take life too seriously and always do what you love.

Candice Hein, Midfield,
Clemson University

No matter what is going on in your personal life, when you get to practice you can forget about all of it for a couple of hours and just work hard. It was like an escape from all the stress in high school.

Brittanie Waddell, Forward/Midfield,
Iowa State University

That sometimes when a person of higher authority is on your case, it doesn't mean they are yelling at you or upset with you, it might mean they are pushing you harder because they know you have more talent and potential inside you.

Christina Metzker, Forward/Midfield,
James Madison University

I don't think I will ever be late for anything in my life. I'm very punctual because of my coach. I make sure I give myself enough time to get to places so I'm there five to ten minutes early. Also, I'm very competitive because of my coach. We were a very determined team and weren't used to losing.

Erin McDowell, Midfield,
Iowa State University

 *To the Parent of a Future Collegiate Player*

As your daughter's advocate, biggest fan, keeper of the house rules, academic guardian, and soccer broker, finding a coach who exemplifies integrity, respect, and trust and who can impart the life lessons of hard work, integrity, professionalism, perseverance, and having a positive attitude can only promote her development on and off the soccer field. I am wowed by the impact these coaches had on their players.

 *To the Future Collegiate Player*

Always remember, soccer is more than just a game; it is the vehicle to opportunity and growth regardless of whether you play in college. Soccer, like all sports, will shape your experiences and interactions; soccer will shape your view of the world and ultimately you. You will be forever changed by your experiences in soccer.

Life Lessons Learned

Work Ethic

- Work hard.
- Value teamwork.
- Have passion and pride.
- Find balance between your personal life and soccer.
- Do it right the first time.
- Finish what you start.
- Be proud of your accomplishments.
- Have fun during the process.

Integrity

- Demand excellence of yourself.
- Be vocal.
- You are in control of yourself.
- Your family is what is most important.
- Be a good person.
- Service is important.
- Character on and off the field.
- Loyalty.
- Do it for you.
- Never pick favorites.
- Listen to your conscience.

Professionalism

- Be a good sport.
- Adapt to many situations.
- Be punctual.
- Treat others with respect.
- Tolerate differences.
- Accept criticism.
- First impressions are important.
- The cream always rises.
- Don't burn bridges.

Perseverance

- Life is not fair.
- There is always politics.
- Be patient.
- Don't fear success.
- Never give up.
- When you fall, it's nice to have friends around.

Mental

- Stay focused.
- Have a positive attitude.
- Don't take it too seriously.
- Let things go, leave it on the field.
- Step up or step away.
- Talents are a gift.
- Motivate yourself.
- Competition is everywhere.

Teammates

Look for players who have the same level of commitment and desires. Find a team that has great chemistry among players. Sometimes the team with the best players may not be the best team. Soccer is a team sport, so if you can find girls that love to play together and push each other, that will be the best team in the end.

Amy Holst, Midfield,
Ball State University

Amy's quote speaks of commitment, shared goals, camaraderie, and support among and between players. All things that make a team a team; all things that make it fun to go to practice; all things that make it tolerable to sacrifice a school dance for an out of town tournament; all things that must occur for players to feel valued, accepted, and a part of something special and meaningful.

⚽ *To the Future Collegiate Player*

Finding a team where you can be happy also equates to performance. If you are not happy, you will not perform at the level you are capable. If the team dynamics are such that factions exist, your ability to focus on soccer may be compromised. Your focus may shift from development and achievement to a preoccupation with personal rivalries among players.

Your club soccer team should be a place where you can go and liberate yourself from the day—a respite from all the normal teenage worries: boys, girls, school, homework assignments and tests, teachers, parents, and friends; a place where common goals coexist with personal success. If it is not, it might be time to reevaluate your team. It might be time to ask yourself if you are getting what you need from the team. Here are some questions to ask yourself:

- Do the majority of the players have the same goals as me?
- Does everyone attend practice regularly?
- Does everyone work hard during practice?
- Is soccer fun?
- Am I progressing?

I asked players: "How many club teams did you play on?" and "If you changed teams, why?" For the first question, I have one of those neat little boxes of data for you. In reviewing the data, there are no significant differences in how many teams a player played on between divisions. It looks like the majority of all players played on two teams.

Number of Club Teams	DI	DII	DIII
1	26%	18%	26%
2	43%	45%	26%
3	15%	19%	20%
4	10%	9%	17%
>4	6%	9%	11%

I was able to categorize the responses to the second part of the question into eight reasons, four of which are self-explanatory: disbanded/merged, moved, switched to a girl's team, and to play with friends, and four that I will expand on: needed something different, philosophy, politics, and miscellaneous.

Something Different

Players talked about changing to a new team because they needed something different for their particular goals. They needed a better team, better training, a higher-level team, more exposure, a well-known coach, and a team that was more focused.

I played one season with a local club team
where I felt I wasn't developing as a player and

then decided to commute to a well-known, well-respected club where I was surrounded by players who were just as good as me or better.

Amanda Garcia, Midfield,
Clemson University

Philosophy

Many players switched teams because the overall philosophy of the team did not fit theirs. They talked about the coach, the commitment to the sport, the team dynamics, the inability to play other sports, and not being treated fairly. Many of the reasons players left their teams appear to mimic what players articulated as important in the section on the coach.

Politics

The focus of all responses here was on team, parents, and the coach's politics. They reached a point where they just could not continue on the team, given the politics.

Miscellaneous

Players mentioned they had to drive too far to practices and needed a closer team, zone restrictions, or they followed their coach to another team.

Players' Advice about Finding a Club Team

I asked players, "What advice would you give a girl who wants to play college soccer about finding a club team?" and I think the best way to represent their responses is to simply share some of their quotes with you. I have tried to organize them somewhat, but they cross over into many different areas. They simply had so much great advice I have tried not to edit out parts of their quotes to keep them in a particular category. Enjoy!

Competitive

> Look for any and every opportunity to play at the highest level possible. This will help you develop and give you the chance and drive to play with and against the best. As far as club teams go, be willing to sacrifice. Be willing to travel for practices and give up long weekends to play at tournaments. Playing for a club team and in college is hard work, so give yourself every edge possible.
>
> *Anonymous,*
> *University of Georgia*

> If you want to play in college, try to play on a premier team. I know that most of the girls either pay their way to success or they earn it. For most of my years I had to play on a lower-division team. College coaches are now recognizing that talent isn't always in the premier league. If you have the resources to do so, I recommend playing on a premier team because, for the most part, the playing level is significantly better.
>
> *Jamie Black, Forward/Midfield,*
> *California State Polytechnic–Pomona*

It all depends on the level you want to play in college. If you want to go DI, play for the best team in the city. If you are going DII or DIII, I don't think it matters as much.

Anonymous,
University of West Florida

I would tell a girl to figure out what she wants to do and go from there. But always remember to work hard at any level she is at.

Jamie Timmons, Midfield,
Slippery Rock University

My best advice would be to challenge yourself. Surround yourself with people just as good, or even better than you. You will learn competition this way and it will get you to the next level.

Anonymous,
West Virginia University

Find a club team that will prepare you physically, mentally, and emotionally. Playing shouldn't be the easiest thing you do, so find a team that will challenge you and help you grow as a player and a person.

Jillian Laydon, Midfield,
Northern State University

It depends on what division a girl wants to play. If they think they want to play DI, then I would suggest they get on the most competitive and skilled team they can find. They will improve their skills by playing with players that are better than them and they will get a taste of the intensity and competition that will exist in DI. If they want to play DII or DIII, then I suggest they find a team that is competitive but not cutthroat. They should find a team with girls they can become friends with and a team they can have fun on while playing good soccer.

Kathryn Austgen, Defense,
Colby College

Find a team that you enjoy playing with because that will show through in how you play. Also, find a team with good enough players so that your team gets looked at by the college coaches.

Candice Hein, Midfield,
Clemson University

Get on the best team that you can, work your you-know-what off, and play your best. You don't have to be the leading scorer to get on a team. It helps, but Mia Hamm needs someone to pass her the ball just like everyone else.

Elizabeth Davis, Forward/Striker,
Manchester College

Showcase Tournaments

If you are looking for a top DI team then I suggest finding a strong club team. A strong team means they will win and get invited to all sorts of events where college coaches will be there to watch. Also, if you have several good players on your team, then coaches are more likely to come watch your games so they can see a lot of talent at once, kind of like killing two birds with one stone.

Joni Vickers, Forward/Midfield,
University of Georgia

Finding a club team is crucial. A coach who takes her/his team to tournaments where college coaches are present on the sidelines is important. Visibility and getting your name out there is a key factor. A girl who wants to play college soccer needs to do her homework on finding an appropriate team and work hard on and off the field because nothing comes without effort.

Anonymous,
Providence College

Find a team that is competitive and travels around *a lot* so you will get noticed more. The better your club team is, the more college coaches are going to pay attention and want to recruit you.

Rebecca Callen, Midfield/Defense,
Bloomsburg University

If you are truly an exceptional athlete, then play for a successful team that travels to the biggest tournaments so you can get a lot of looks by coaches, because they are always looking.

Anonymous,
University of North Carolina–Pembroke

Finding a good, competitive club team is really hard to do, especially if you aren't the cream-of-the-crop soccer player. It is very difficult to find a team with eighteen or more committed girls as well. If you want to play college soccer, you are going to have to find a team that has its name known and plays and wins a lot of showcase tournaments. I did not play on one of those teams and I never got recruited. I took it upon myself to contact schools. The best advice I can give is not to wait to be recruited. College coaches are very busy and do not have time to scout everywhere. If you want to play soccer, call or e-mail the coach. Not only will it get your foot in the door, it will show coaches that you have initiative, and that is always a plus. I can't emphasize enough; do not wait to be recruited.

Cori Shepler, Midfield,
Clarion University

Good Fit

You need to find a balance. You need a popular club team that will get to the important tournaments but is not politically run and that is fun to play for. Now, this is a very hard thing to do, but you need to decide if it's exposure you want or actual fun soccer.

Kate Lowe, Forward,
East Carolina University

Find a team who really wants to go to the next level and play college soccer. You need to be on a team that loves soccer and loves to come to practice and play in games. Your team should go to a lot of tournaments that really expose everyone to college coaches.

Melissa Penney, Forward,
East Carolina University

Make sure you find a team that you fit into soccer-wise and non-soccer-wise.

Anonymous,
University of Houston

Don't play on a team that is die-hard, hardcore soccer. You don't want to get so burned out of playing while growing up that you don't want to play when you are older. Try to find a happy medium.

Kara Carlile, Forward/Midfield,
Murray State University

Play for a competitive team, but don't lose sight of high school teammates/friends, because high school athletics can be so important.

Betsy Pratt,
St. Cloud State

Find a team where your attitude toward playing soccer and toward life is mirrored, or at the very least, respected by the coach. If your coach's only priority is winning, and your main priority is to develop as a player, you're probably not going to have a meaningful experience playing for that individual. It is also important that you can feel comfortable with the team's ideals. If your teammates are more interested in partying than in coming to practice ready to work, and you feel differently, perhaps this team is not the one for you. At the same time, if your teammates live for this team and this team alone, yet you are attempting to balance your club team and, for example, another high school sport, you will probably feel the effects of such a compromise through diminished playing time, criticism from your teammates, and pressure to prioritize in favor of the club team. Find a team where you can get what you want out of the experience. Find a team with a coach that you can respect and who can respect you, a coach that will develop you as a player and a person.

Kristen Werder, Forward,
Clarion University of Pennsylvania

Find a team that will be traveling to tournaments. Most of all, though, find a coach that you are happy playing for. They will either teach you the world or make your world a living #!#! I have moved between many, many teams in my time and had to deal with a great deal of soccer politics. Girls' teams especially are hard because if they have been together for a long period of time they can be very cliquish. A good group of players will accept new players. The best team I played for was the Pickering Power Rebels from Ontario, Canada, as a guest player at the USA Cup. Even though he had never seen me play, the coach was excited to have me. The girls were all willing to have a new player play with them.

They were excited to meet and play with someone new. Even though I didn't really get to practice with them all that much, there was a great deal of support from the coach, players, and parents. They were serious about playing soccer, but also had fun. Balance is key!

Amy Arundale, Forward,
Haverford College

Development

Don't just play on a team because you are the best player, leading scorer, or top defender. Get on a team that challenges you to develop as a player and person. I went to a team where I didn't know anyone, but it was the best decision I made. Make sure the coach is good and that they want to teach you. Get something out of every practice. You are there for the soccer learning experience. Get on a team where girls want to be just as serious as you. Almost all of the girls I played soccer with went on to play college.

Anonymous,
University of Indianapolis

Find a club team that focuses on the needs of each player, not parents or a board of directors. Find a team that will challenge you to be better, but also allows you to help make others better.

Anonymous,
Stonehill College

Don't pick the club team by color, or who's on it, pick it by the coaches and trainers. Make sure they work with you one on one and can demonstrate every drill, not just tell you. Practices should be an intense workout, not a waste of time or a get-together.

Becky Imhoff, Forward/Midfield,
University of Cincinnati

Soccer Camps and Tournaments

Hold On to Your Wallet!

> Many colleges have camps for kids of all ages. Although these camps may be more expensive, it is the easiest way for young players to get recognized by that particular college. If a coach likes a player and her talent or hard work at this age, there is no reason why that coach wouldn't follow her progression as she gets closer to the recruiting process.
>
> *Amanda Garcia, Midfield,*
> *Clemson University*

Introduction

There are an abundance of soccer camps and tournaments offered throughout the year across the country. If you're from Wisconsin, like me, going to a tournament in sunny San Diego in late November always seems like a good idea; however, careful considerations of the goals for attending a tournament or camp are crucial so one's life savings don't dwindle to pennies over the course of a season.

Being a part of a competitive club team or the Olympic Development Program (ODP) requires a certain amount of travel to camps and tournaments. This travel can encompass the state and beyond. On some occasions it may dictate getting on a plane. Yes, exciting, but expensive. Recreational teams usually attend local camps and tournaments, but this can add up too if one doesn't discriminate.

Being a smart consumer is paramount given the choices and pressures to attend tournaments and camps (usually from your daughter whose best friend is going to an overnight camp and invited her to be her roommate!).

Beyond the logistical and financial considerations, soccer camps and tournaments are a great way for your daughter to compare her soccer abilities against other players, develop and refine her skills, make new friends, gain some independence (in a very controlled environment), and meet and work with current collegiate players and coaches.

In this chapter I will articulate the kinds of camps and tournaments available, give you guidance in how to choose and when to attend them, and offer insight into what the goals should be for the U-8 versus the U-14 player. Data will also be presented from my survey on how many camps the collegiate players attended and their results when they attended a camp purely for the exposure to a collegiate coach.

Camps

In the world of soccer camps, there are at least four types: day camps, overnight camps, skills camps, and ODP regional camp. Associated with each type of camp is a financial commitment, where need-based scholarships may or may not be available. Always ask!

Day Camps

Day camps may range anywhere from one to five days in length and can convene all day or just for the morning or afternoon. Day camps are usually the least expensive compared to overnight camps. Some of the best camps my two daughters ever attended were local day camps where current female collegiate athletes from our own city worked. These types of camps focus on skill development, tactical play, and positioning. Players are usually given a commemorative T-shirt and a ball from the camp.

Day camps are especially appropriate for the beginning soccer player and also for the advanced player. They increase in intensity level given the age and skill level of the group. All the day camps I have watched share one important ingredient: fun. Everyone—coaching staff and players—appears to be having a great time.

Overnight Camps

Overnight camps typically range from three to five days in length and are the most expensive because they are feeding and housing the players. These camps also work on skill development, tactical play, and positioning, but they also might add something like nutrition, one-on-one assessments, written evaluations, and collegiate advice. Players usually receive a commemorative T-shirt and a ball.

Overnight camps are appropriate for older players only. Some overnight camps can be pretty intense and highly structured, depending on their focus, while others may be more lighthearted and loosely structured. The feedback I have gotten from players about overnight camps is that they require a great deal of hard work, but they are very fun.

Skills Camps

Skills camps normally are shorter in length (usually three-plus days), can range from partial to full days, and can even require an overnight stay. Their cost may range from pretty inexpensive to moderately priced, if the camp is overnight. Skills camps focus on one type of skill or player. For example, goalie camps for goalies or shooting camps for forwards. Some are more generic in that they may focus on technical skill development for all field players. Players are usually given a commemorative T-shirt and sometimes a ball.

Skills camps are appropriate for all ages; however, if they are overnight, I wouldn't recommend sending a U-8er, as her parents will inevitably be called to pick her up in the middle of the night. Again, the feedback I have gotten from players, along with my two daughters' experiences, is that skills camps are both fun and educational.

ODP Regional Camp

This is an invitational camp for players in the state who have made the state Olympic Development Team. It is five days long and pretty pricey. Its focus is to pick players for the regional pool team, so its intensity level is high. At ODP camp there is goalie training, skill development, tactical field training, nutrition, sports psychology, and lectures and advice on collegiate play. Players are given daily feedback and a formal written evaluation at the end of camp. They are evaluated by a multitude of collegiate coaches. Thus, exposure to college coaches is excellent. Players are given a commemorative T-shirt and a ball, and if they have been to camp before, they bring a T-shirt of their own to trade for another player's T-shirt (preferably from a player out of state).

The youngest players that attend ODP camp are the U-13ers. Most players do not like this camp, as the intensity level is overwhelming, the evaluations can be brutal, and the competition is tough. This camp is emotionally demanding, similar to playing in Division I.

Attending a Camp for the Exposure

As you identify soccer programs and colleges in which you are interested, you may choose to strategically attend that college's summer soccer camp to get exposure to the coach. In my survey, I asked players, "Did you ever attend a camp because you knew a particular coach would be there? If so, was it worthwhile?" The data are presented in the table below.

Attended Camp for Exposure	DI	DII	DIII
Yes	46%	23%	32%
Was it worthwhile?	88%	39%	94%

It appears that players who went to a DI program used this strategy the most and found it to be very worthwhile. Although DIII players used this strategy less, they found it more worthwhile than the DI players. DII players used this strategy the least of all three divisions, and found it least worthwhile.

If you decide to try this strategy, make sure the person you are going to see is actually going to be there. Just because it is his or her camp doesn't always mean he or she will be on site. Throughout the summer, college coaches attend ODP camp and travel to tournaments to watch potential recruits.

What to Look for in a Camp

I asked players: "How many soccer camps did you attend throughout your youth career?" The data is represented in the table below. The largest numbers within each division are: 28% of DI players attended more than ten camps, 32% of DII players attended four to six camps, and 31% of DIII players attended one to three camps. I don't know if there is a correlation between how many camps a player attended and which collegiate division they chose, but it appears that DI players attended the most camps, followed by DII players, and then DIII players. I think the question is: Did DI players attend the most camps in order to be competitive for DI? These were pretty astonishing numbers.

Number of Camps	DI	DII	DIII
0	22%	12%	7%
1-3	14%	24%	31%
4-6	18%	32%	17%
7-10	18%	14%	19%
>10	28%	18%	26%

 *To All Parents*

Given the percentage of players who attended more than ten camps, being a smart consumer is very important. Here are some questions to think about as you decide between camps:

- Who's training and teaching? What are their credentials?
- What are the goals of the camp?

- Are the activities well planned? What is the agenda?
- How much downtime is there?
- Is there appropriate supervision?
- What do other players/parents who have attended this camp say?
- What is the ratio between players and coaches?
- Will your daughter get individual attention?
- Is there an evaluation of players at the end of camp?

Tournaments

Attending tournaments can provide a player with healthy competition, camaraderie, a sense of being a part of something exciting, new friendships, and travels to new cities and states. The downside to tournaments is, of course, the expense and time.

Tournaments, both in and out of state, can be expensive. Out-of-state tournaments usually include overnight stays of anywhere between two and five nights in a hotel, food, and travel expenses. With some tournaments, travel expenses mean airfare! The local tournaments can add up financially as well, with the food and the booths that sell cute hair scrunchies, soccer blankets, new cleats, and a multitude of other soccer paraphernalia.

Similar to the variety and number of camps there are to choose from, there are tournaments for every level of competitiveness. There are tournaments for entire teams, partial teams, and newly formed teams; for one day's duration through five days; indoor or outdoor, and some tournaments exist solely for the purpose of collegiate recruiting. Some tournaments have pools for players who need to find a team.

Tournament options can be found in subscriptions such as *Soccer America* or on the Internet if you search by region. Most teams attend tournaments based on their club's recommendation or word of mouth. Listed below are the types of tournament opportunities available for players.

Recreational Tournaments

Recreational tournaments are non-competitive, meaning the focus is on fun, working as a team, and enjoying the sport, all within the context of the game. Winning is secondary to satisfaction and enjoyment. Recreational tournaments are suitable for all age groups, but not all teams. Teams that are identified as premier, select, or competitive should not participate.

Competitive Tournaments

Competitive tournaments are just that: competitive. The focus of each team is on winning and being a strong opponent. Fun, satisfaction, and enjoyment are secondary to winning and the competition itself. Teams that are recreational should not participate in competitive tournaments unless the goal is to determine if a more competitive level is appropriate for the team.

3v3's, 5v5's, 8v8's

These tournaments compete with only three players, five players, or eight players on the field at one time. The actual playing field is smaller than a regular field. They can be very competitive or recreational. Most players put teams together based on friendships—they can be from different club teams or the same club team—and winning teams usually get the opportunity to compete at a national competition. The benefits of this type of tournament play include lots of playing time for each player and practicing individual skills and ball control, because the playing field is smaller.

Recruiting Tournaments

Recruiting tournaments are for high school juniors and seniors only. College coaches attend for the sole purpose of recruiting players. At recruiting tournaments, players usually have sent coaches their itinerary, inviting the coach to come see them play.

College coaches attend recruiting tournaments to watch multiple players and to identify other potential recruits. A parent representative from the team will usually have collected soccer résumés for each player to hand out to interested coaches. College coaches may approach players they are interested in and begin a dialogue. Although the focus of the recruiting tournament is not on winning, the competitive spirit is in the air as players try to showcase their individual talents while competing against other teams.

Given the goal of this type of tournament, it is very important to always be at the top of your game. Coaches attend these tournaments to watch many players, so the actual time allotted to watch your game may be limited to a few minutes. You will not know when they are watching you!

Goals for Attending Tournaments Broken Down by Age and Focus

U-13 and Under

For the younger teams, attending tournaments should be about the fun and excitement of meeting and playing other teams. Players should take away from the experience a sense of accomplishment, confidence, and a bit more of an awareness of field positions. The focus at this level should not be about winning.

U-14 and Older

The goals for attending tournaments at U-14 and older become more intense with the older age groups. This is especially true if the goal is to develop players for college. The team must seek out competition at every opportunity and be competitive. It's not about winning; it's about being competitive enough to be a creditable opponent. Within a competitive game, players can showcase their individual talents, their mental determination and toughness, and their knowledge of strategic play. Below I have broken down the goals based on year in high school.

Freshman and Sophomore Year

A freshman or sophomore in high school should attend the most competitive tournaments her club team can attend. She will develop into a better player through playing better players. This will also give her feedback regarding her skills and abilities in comparison to other players.

Junior Year

Junior year in high school is a very important year. Attending tournaments during and after one's junior year can be key to getting recruited. Players should send their letter of interest, résumé, and tournament schedule to coaches they want to come see them play. College coaches are attending tournaments scouting and recruiting players. Although a coach is not able to initiate conversation with a junior in high school yet, they can watch and wait!

Senior Year

The summer after one's junior year is when players should begin attending recruiting tournaments. Players should still be attending recruiting tournaments in the fall of their senior year as well. Because coaches often approach players and begin recruiting them at these tournaments, players must be age-appropriate. After these tournaments, players usually receive letters from coaches expressing interest.

I'm certainly not aware of all the recruiting tournaments there are; however, I do know of a few local ones in the Midwest and a few of the big-name ones. Three local tournaments in my area that were excellent for recruiting were the College Search Kickoff in Muscatine, Iowa; the USA Cup in Blaine, Minnesota; and the All American Girls, also in Blaine, Minnesota.

The big-name tournaments, WAGS (Washington Area Girls Soccer), in Washington, D.C., Surf Cup, in San Diego, California; the Dallas Cup, in Dallas, Texas; and Raleigh, in North Carolina usually attract more top-tier D1 coaches and are very competitive. Don't worry if your team doesn't get invited to these. Yes, some are invitation only.

Divisions I, II, and III
Three Levels, Three Lifestyles

Take your time and really think about what you want in a college, and I mean outside of soccer. Big or small? Good football team? Academics? Social life? Every detail is important because this is your future and where you could be spending the next four to five years of your life. Make sure you make the decision for yourself, not because of something someone else wants (your mom or dad). Just don't let anyone pressure you into anything. Remember this is *your* life, so it's *your* choice.

Joni Vickers, Forward/Midfield,
University of Georgia

Introduction

With the three divisions of college soccer come three distinct levels of commitment and lifestyle. Knowing what your goals are, both athletically and academically, will help you determine for which lifestyle and division you are best suited.

This chapter is about providing you with the tools you need to make the right decision for you. Included in this chapter are a Soccer Survey and Academic Questionnaire and statistics about how much time and effort are required in preseason, in season, and spring season for all three divisions. Advice from collegiate players is sprinkled throughout this chapter to assist you in deciding which division is right for you.

The Soccer Survey is designed to help you define how big a part you want soccer to play in your college life. It assesses such things as how much time commitment you are willing to spend practicing and playing soccer in and out of season, how much you are willing to push yourself to perfect your soccer skills, whether an athletic scholarship is important, and how much travel you are willing to do.

The Academic Questionnaire is designed to help you clarify what you would like from a college or university. For example, the optimal size of classroom for your learning, academic majors available, whether the school has a football team, whether it's important to be located near a big city or in the country, and academic rigor.

By working through the Soccer Survey and Academic Questionnaire and all the statistics in this chapter, you will have all the knowledge you need to make an educated decision. But there is one more thing to consider when making this decision: your heart. Herein rests the caveat to this entire chapter: all good decisions are tempered by the heart. What does this mean? It means that your heart—the feelings inside you—must always be considered. Good decisions are based on both the objective (data) and the subjective (your heart). Your heart will be addressed at the end of the book in the chapter on Choosing the Right School and

Team: It's Like Falling in Love. For now, let us stick with the tangibles: the data, and you making some concrete decisions about your academic and athletic career.

 To the Future Collegiate Player

The Soccer Survey and Academic Questionnaire are meant to help you identify and clarify your feelings, thoughts, and desires. Please take them in a quiet place, away from distractions and others' opinions.

 To the Parent of a Future Collegiate Player

Your role in this chapter is to review the survey and the questionnaire once your daughter has completed them and listen to her reasoning and decisions. If and when she questions her decisions or begins looking at schools that don't meet her established criteria, gently encourage her to review her completed survey and questionnaire and ask if her feelings have changed. Try to withhold your opinion. Listen and ask clarifying questions, nod and smile. She may need to talk this out and the best way she can do this is by bouncing her thoughts off of you.

Additionally, your goal in this chapter is to familiarize yourself with the three divisions and lifestyles. With the information I have provided, you will be able to help your daughter when she has questions or concerns.

Soccer Survey

The Soccer Survey is comprised of nine sets of three statements for each area of assessment, including money, time commitment, intensity, travel, balance, and academics. For each set of three sentences, check the one that most sounds like you. Be honest with yourself when you are answering the Soccer Survey. Your future happiness depends on it!

Check only *one* sentence in each area.

Intensity

1_____I think soccer practice in college should be *very* intense, serious, and competitive.

2_____I think soccer practice in college should be *somewhat* intense, serious, and competitive.

3_____I think soccer practice in college should be *a little* intense, serious, and competitive.

Money

1_____It is a priority to me to attend a school that offers a *large* amount of athletic scholarships.

2_____It is a priority to me to attend a school that offers *some* athletic scholarship money.

3_____It is *not* a priority to me to receive an athletic scholarship at all.

Travel

1_____I am willing to give up *all* my weekends during the season to either travel out of town for games or to participate in team events for home games.

2_____I am willing to give up *some* of my weekends during the season to travel out of town for games.

3_____I am willing to give up a *few* of my weekends during the season to travel out of town for games.

Time in preseason

1_____I am willing to devote *eight or more* hours a day to preseason.

2_____I am willing to devote *six or more* hours a day to preseason.

3_____I am willing to devote *four or more* hours a day to preseason.

Time in season

1_____I am willing to devote *three or more* hours a day, *six days* per week, plus games during the season.

2_____I am willing to devote *two or more* hours a day, *five days* per week, plus games during the season.

3_____I am willing to devote *two or more* hours a day, *four to five days* per week, plus games during the season.

Time over winter

1______I am willing to devote *eight or more* hours a week to training over the winter months.

2______I am willing to devote *six or more* hours a week to training over the winter months.

3______I am willing to devote *four or more* hours a week over the winter months.

Time in spring season

1______I am willing to devote *ten or more* hours a week to soccer during spring season.

2______I am willing to devote *eight or more* hours a week to soccer during the spring season.

3______I am willing to devote *a little time* to playing soccer during the spring season.

Mandatory team community and campus volunteerism

1______ I am willing to devote a *good amount* of time all year to service and campus functions.

2______I am willing to devote a *little time*, here and there, to service and campus functions.

3______I am willing to devote a *very small* amount of time to service and campus functions.

Academics

1______I am willing to take *a reduced* class load and possibly *delay my graduation* one year so I can devote more time to soccer.

2_____I am willing to *reduce* my class load just *a little* and possibly *graduate one semester later* so I can devote more time to soccer.

3_____I am *not* willing to *reduce* my class load and delay graduation so I can devote more time to soccer.

Balance

1_____I am willing to have soccer be the *main part* of my college experience.

2_____I want soccer to be an *equal part* of my college experience along with academics and the social experience.

3_____I want my *main focus to be academics* in college but I still want to include soccer in my college life as well as the social experience.

To score the Soccer Survey:

1) Count how many statements in the number one position you have and write it here:_______

2) Count how many statements in the number two position you have and write it here:______

3) Count how many statements in the number three position you have and write it here:______

4) Which position has the most points?______

- If you have the most points in *position one*, then you may be well suited for a Division I program.

- If you have the most points in *position two*, then you may be well suited for a Division II program.

- If you have the most points for *position three*, then you may be well suited for a Division III program.

- Now, I want you to go back to the survey and review the categories with the knowledge that sentence one corresponds to DI, sentence two corresponds to DII, and sentence three corresponds to DIII.

1) Are you willing to change any of your answers now that you know some key information about the commitment levels for DI, DII, and DIII?
Yes_______No_______

2) Are you willing to entertain a different division than what you originally scored on the Soccer Survey?
Yes_______No_______

If you answered *No* to both of the two questions above, then you have a preliminary idea of which division of soccer is appropriate for you. The following data in this chapter should help you verify your choice.

If you answered *Yes* to both of the two questions above, then you have an inner conflict to resolve. The data in this chapter will help you determine your priorities and commitment level.

If you answered *Yes* to either question above and *No* to the other question, then you have an inner conflict to resolve. The data in this chapter will help you determine your priorities and commitment level.

*The Soccer Survey generalizes some of the differences between Divisions I, II, and III to highlight what you may typically encounter in programs. There are always exceptions and they usually occur in the top programs within each division. For example, some top DII and DIII programs may be just as intense as a DI programs.

Lifestyle and Commitment Differences between DI, DII, and DIII

> It is a lot more work than you think; when I signed I didn't realize it is a job. It is a full-time commitment, especially if you want to make it to the top at a good program. Every day you will wake up and have something dealing with soccer, be it speed training, lifting, or practice. You will have to make a lot of sacrifices to play (no big parties during season, managing your time well). Sometimes your body will just hurt

so bad during preseason and you will want to quit, but you have to keep going.

Anonymous,
Wright State University

There are important differences between each division with regard to length of preseason; training activities in season; winter and spring season; and volunteer and community service commitments. I have created three charts, one for each division, for you to analyze.

As you compare each chart, you will notice a difference between DI and the other two divisions with regard to time. For example, the length of preseason is at least one week longer than DII and DIII programs, during winter and spring season there are required obligations such as fundraising and community service, and "in season" there are mandatory team events after games (even if your parents are visiting for the weekend; your parents are usually not invited).

As you review the charts, the following definitions will help you decipher the activities:

- Fitness = Cooper test, timed team runs of two or more miles, fifteen seconds of fun, fartleks
- Technical = foot skills, headers, drills, trapping, etc.
- Lift = weight training
- Individuals = coaches work with each athlete one-on-one
- Exhibition games = team plays other schools not in conference during preseason.

Division I				
	Preseason	**Season**	**Winter**	**Spring**
Duration	2-4 weeks	10+ weeks	6-8+ weeks	8+ weeks
Time	2-3 sessions daily, 8 hours per day, 6 days per week	3+ hours per day	2+ hours per day, 4+ days per week	2+ hours per day, 5 days per week
Training	Fitness, team building, scrimmages, drills, exhibition games	Fitness, scrimmages, drills, lift, technical, small-sided games, individuals	Fitness, lift, small-sided games, individuals	Tournaments, scrimmage other schools, fitness, technical, lift
Community Service and Volunteerism	n/a	Mandatory dinner with various school dignitaries	Soup kitchen, soccer camps, pledge-a-thon, concessions at basketball games	High school preseason clinic, mini-camps at local schools, work track meets timing events

Division II				
	Preseason	**Season**	**Winter**	**Spring**
Duration	2-3 weeks	10 weeks	*2-10 weeks	*2-12 weeks
Time	2-3 sessions per day, 6 plus hours, 5 days per week	4-5 practices per week, 2 hours per day	2 hours per day, 2-3 days per week	2 hours per day, 2-4 days per week
Training	Fitness, fitness test, fun fitness, scrimmages, drills, skill development, 1v1, plyometrics, swim	Fitness, lift, drills, skill development, scrimmages, technical, small-sided games	Scrimmages, weight train, fitness	Scrimmage other schools, personal training, run, lift
Community Service and Volunteerism	n/a	n/a	Mini-camps for K-6, holiday gifts for the needy	Soccer clinics, community fundraisers

* The variability in duration of time—two to ten weeks for winter and two to twelve weeks for spring season—stems from how schools define winter and spring season. Some schools consider winter season to be the two weeks before winter break, and spring season begins when the students return from break sometime in January and ends in May or June, when school ends. Other schools define winter season as January through March and spring season as April through the end of the school year.

Division III				
	Preseason	**Season**	**Winter**	**Spring**
Duration	2-3 weeks	8+ weeks	0-4 weeks	0-4 weeks
Time	2 sessions per day, 4+ hours, 5 days per week	4-5 practices per week, 2 hours per day	1-2 hours per day, 2 days per week	1-2 hours per week, 2 days per week
Training	Fitness, fitness test, scrimmages, drills, skill development, agility training, team bonding, exhibition games	Team training, fitness, lift, scrimmages, long runs	Train on own, indoor games, lift, fitness	Lift, run, scrimmages
Community Service and Volunteerism	n/a	n/a	n/a	Clean up parks, plant trees, clinics for local kids

Academic Questionnaire

I picked the college because of its size. I am not a big-city girl, so I did not want to attend a huge school. I also picked this school because of the nursing program and because of the weather.

Jen Mascarin, Midfield,
University of South Carolina-Aiken

The college had a good academic reputation and lots of educational programs I was interested in. The environment seemed one I could fit into and soccer seemed like a perfect bonus.

Sara Fick, Forward,
Bloomsburg University

Honestly, I picked this school because I liked the state of South Carolina and it was close to the first school I played at. Also, I was dating someone when I left my old school so I tried to stay close. *Big mistake.* After I left my first school, I wish I would have looked around a lot more and been open to other places.

Audie Beckman, Forward,
University of South Carolina-Aiken

The Academic Questionnaire assesses the other element of your decision-making process, the academic side of the equation. Whether you choose DI, DII, or DIII for soccer, the academic factor is integral to your happiness within your major of study and your professional endeavors beyond college. After all, it is why you are going to college!

By identifying what is important to you in a college, you

will be able to reduce the number of schools you review and consider. Picking a school for the academic characteristics *and* its soccer attributes can be overwhelming. However, if you know, for example, you want a rural setting, you can cross off all schools that are in an urban/city area. If it is important to be within driving distance from home, then you can cross off all schools that are farther away than you are willing to drive.

In addition to variables such as distance and location, the Academic Questionnaire will highlight other important considerations when reviewing schools, such as classroom size, a competitive academic program, financial reciprocity, and personal preferences such as the school having a football team or a Greek system.

1)　The size of school I am interested in attending is: (check one)

______Very Small (3,000 students or less)

______Small (3,000–10,000)

______Medium (10,000–20,000)

______Large (over 20,000)

2)　The type of setting I want my school to be near or in is: (check one)

______Rural/Country

______Urban/City

______Don't really care

3)   The type of campus I am interested in is:
        (check one)

______Picturesque, with lots of grass and trees

______More concrete so it's easy to get around

______Don't really care

4)   The location of my school can be as far away
        from home as: (check one)

______1–2 hours away

______3–5 hours away

______6–8 hours away

______9 or more hours away

5)   I am looking for a particular level of academic
        competitiveness: (check one)

______Not very competitive

______Somewhat competitive

______Very competitive

* Question five will depend on your major, how competitive
your field is for job placement, and if you plan to attend
graduate school.

6)   I am interested in schools that have the following
        list of majors: (list your current interests)

________________________   ________________________

________________________   ________________________

________________________   ________________________

*You may not know exactly what you want to be in life yet, but jot down some ideas.

7)   It is important that my college offer the following other sports/activities:
______Greek system
______Football
______Hockey
______Men's soccer
Other___________________________________

8)   I learn best in classroom sizes that are small (under forty students):
______True
______False

* In this environment you are able to talk to your professors and participate in group discussions during class.

9)   It doesn't really matter if my classroom size is large (over 100 students):
______True
______False

* In a larger environment, you may not get to know your professor or participate in group discussions with your professors. Group discussions are normally led by teaching assistants after lectures have ended.

10)   Financially, I am able to attend a school out of
       state:
_______Yes

_______No

11) My state has reciprocity with_________________

* Reciprocity means there is an agreement between two or more states to accept the other state's students and only charge in-state tuition. So you can attend an out-of-state school and pay your state's tuition only. You can check into whether your state has a reciprocity agreement by doing a Google search or reviewing your state university's website.

Now that you have completed the Academic Questionnaire, keep it handy to refer back to when comparing schools and soccer programs. You may also want to rank your top three "must haves, will not budge on" items.

The Emotional Component

I initially started playing at a DI school because I thought that was where I wanted to be. But I transferred to a DII school after my first semester. My DI coach did not care about me as a person or my education. He was all about winning. My DII coach is awesome. He asks me about myself all the time. He keeps after me about my grades. Not just me, but the whole team. I picked this school because I really liked the way the coach talked to me as a person first, then as a player. I was a person to him, not just another soccer player.

Laura Crews, Forward,
Pfeiffer University

There is a body of research that suggests females respond positively to people in various situations when they believe they are liked and when there is a positive emotional connection. I asked players the following set of questions to see if there were any differences between the three divisions of soccer in terms of intensity of their program and how they perceive their coach's feelings for them. By intensity, I mean players being pushed to excel beyond their normal boundaries, having great demands placed on their emotions and physicality, and a soccer environment that is highly competitive and selective regarding playing time.

I asked players about the intensity level of their programs and if their head coach cares about them personally and academically. The data are presented below.

For the first question, "How intense is your soccer program?" players at DI programs rated their programs the highest, "very intense," followed by DII and then DIII. For the category "moderately intense," DIII players reported the highest percentage, followed by DII and then DI. For the category "not very intense" all three divisions of players reported very low percentages, with DI reporting the lowest, followed by DII and then DIII.

Intensity Level of Program	DI	DII	DIII
Very Intense	58%	45%	28%
Moderately Intense	41%	50%	65%
Not Very Intense	1%	5%	7%

The next question was, "Does your head coach care about you?" Players in all three divisions overwhelmingly reported that their head coach cares about them. There were no differences between divisions. For DI and DII, a small percentage reported "not sure." That is interesting!

Does Your Head Coach Care About You?	DI	DII	DIII
Yes	88%	88%	87%
No	8%	6%	13%
Not Sure	4%	6%	0%

The next question was, "Does your head coach care about your education?" Players in all three divisions reported that their head coach cares about their education.

Does Your Head Coach Care About Your Education?	DI	DII	DIII
Yes	96%	95%	94%
No	3%	5%	6%
Not Sure	1%	0%	0%

I asked a fourth question, "Who do you mainly interact with on a daily basis: your head coach, assistant coach and/ or trainers?" because I had heard that in some DI programs, the head coach may interact very little with the players, leaving feedback to the coaching assistants. I thought that if a coach doesn't always interact with players, then the players may interpret that as a lack of caring. The data below indicate that for all divisions, players mainly interact with their head coach although there is considerable overlap with their trainers and assistant coaches.

An interesting aside is that in DI, players interact second most with their trainers on a daily basis. Given the intensity level of DI programs, injuries are prevalent as players push themselves to compete and achieve. Perhaps that's the correlation.

Who Do You Mainly Interact With on a Daily Basis	DI	DII	DIII
Head Coach	90%	92%	94%
Assistant Coach	37%	46%	24%
Trainers	66%	24%	39%

Interestingly, there are no differences between divisions with regard to the emotional connection players feel they have with their coaches and the intensity level of their program. Players in all three divisions rated their head coach as caring about them equally and rated their head coach as caring about their education equally.

I am very surprised by this data in relation to DI. I had always heard that DI was like a business, where head coaches interact very little with their players because they didn't want to have their personal feelings sway their judgment. Given the commitment many DI players give to their program, I am delighted to know they feel their head coach cares about them personally.

Game Plan

Given the number of colleges and universities and soccer programs out there, your goal is to narrow the search and concentrate on finding a good fit between the academics and the soccer. Having taken the Soccer Survey and the Academic Questionnaire, you are ready to assess all schools and soccer programs against the criteria you have deemed important to your college experience.

One of the easiest characteristics to narrow down your search is a school's size. If you have decided a small school is important to you, then eliminate all large programs. Once you have identified schools that meet your size requirement, you can begin to assess each of the remaining schools' other attributes. For example, if you have decided you only want a school that has a football team, then remove any school that does not have a football team. If you have decided you do not want to be more than three to five hours away from home, then discard all programs that are farther away than five hours.

You can also eliminate schools based on division. If you have decided to play Division II, then remove all programs from your list that are either Division I or Division III. I know this is kind of hard—to remove schools you haven't even really reviewed—but if you don't eliminate some schools, the list will be too large to manage and review. Remember, you want to be able to make a well-informed decision based on knowledge, personal preferences, and your academic goals as well as your soccer goals. The only way to do this is to narrow the search.

To find data on schools, you will probably have to review multiple resources. This is going to take time and effort on your part. Do a little bit of research each day and it won't seem so overwhelming. Also, if your parents are willing, they can help with the data collection. Here is a list of resources to get you started:

- High school counselor: Your high school counselor is a great resource. He or she usually will have a lot of brochures from schools and can provide information on different colleges or universities. He or she may also be able to generate a list for you based on school size.

- NCAA website: If you have determined a particular division is right for you, then go to the NCAA website and find its list of schools within each division. They will also have a link for you to click on to go directly to that school's website.

- School website: Once you have identified a school, go directly to its website. Once there, you can identify all the criteria that are important to you.

- *US News & World Report* is a good resource to review individual schools for their academic prowess, school and class size, location, cost, etc. Every year a new listing is created where schools are evaluated and ranked.

- *The Princeton Review* will give you information on schools that are the best value for your money, both public and private.

The High School Years
What Really Matters: Grades!

Make sure you have a good GPA in high school; you don't want to limit yourself just because you have bad grades.

Anonymous,
University of West Florida

It doesn't matter how good a player is if they don't have the high school grades and SAT/ACT scores to clear the Clearinghouse.

Laura Crews, Forward,
Pfeiffer University

Introduction

Your high school years are important to your future as a collegiate athlete. This is such an important statement I need you to read it again: Your high school years are important to your future as a collegiate athlete.

I realize it may be hard to think about college when it's so far away, but the decisions you make today about school and soccer will determine your future. The decisions you make will determine if you are able to attend college, where you attend college, when you attend college, and if you are eligible to play soccer in college.

For the athlete who wants a dual career in college—to play college soccer *and* to get a college degree—commitment, preparation, dedication, and foresight are required. College isn't something you just decide to do one day; playing college soccer isn't something you just decide to do either. Both require effort, talent, and dedication. And it all starts in high school.

It's not up to your high school teachers or your friends, your parents, your club, or high school coach to get you ready for college. It's up to you!

If you have thought about playing college soccer, you have a lot of work to do. The effort you put into preparing yourself for college, getting good grades, researching schools and soccer programs, and finally, making the decision where to go, represent a promise to your goals and dreams.

This chapter outlines, year by year, what you need to do both athletically and academically to achieve your goal of playing college soccer. Academically, you will learn about the national entrance exams you need to take, as well as when to take your school's career inventory and my Academic Questionnaire. Athletically, you will learn when to contact coaches, research programs, register in the NCAA Clearinghouse, make a video, create your résumé, and when to take my Soccer Survey. You will also learn how to prepare yourself academically for the travel, the practices, the games, and the huge time commitment of a college soccer career while maintaining academic eligibility. It all starts in high school and it all begins with your commitment to your academic career first.

Freshman Year

Academically, your freshman year sets the stage for your entire high school career. I don't say this to put pressure on you; I believe having this knowledge as you begin your high school career will enable you to take control of your future.

There are things you can do to ensure your college success, and it starts during your freshman year. I have categorized them into two separate groups: academics and athletics.

Academics

Get good grades. Period! Your freshman grades follow you throughout your high school years and straight to college. They accumulate on your transcript and, over time, develop a picture of you that college admissions administrators and staff see, along with potential coaches. People you don't even know will begin to make decisions about your abilities and whether you belong at their school based on the accumulation of grades on your transcript.

Admissions deans see many essays each year that explain what happened during a student's freshman year in high school. Don't be one of those people who need to include in their essay such statements as:

"My GPA would have been higher if I had been more mature. I didn't realize how important grades were during my freshman year."

Or

"As you can see, there is an upward trend; when I got serious about my grades, they went up."

Or

"If you don't count my freshman year, I have a much higher GPA."

If you begin to focus on academics during your freshman year, you will meet more colleges' admission standards. College admissions committees will open their doors for you and you will have more schools to choose from than you can imagine. Now combine your good GPA with a good score on the ACT or SAT (college entrance exams), and you are set! Schools will recruit you for your mind and may even be willing to give you an academic scholarship. Your only concern will be finding an athletic program that suits you. Trust me; this is the scenario you want to play over and over in your mind.

If you don't focus on your grades, doors will close. Admissions committees will determine you don't make their minimum academic cutoffs and will deny you admittance to their school. Soccer programs may conclude that because your grades from high school are poor, you may become "academically ineligible" to play during your college career. Some programs may choose not to recruit you because they don't want to take a chance on you not being eligible to play. You are no good to a college coach if you are academically ineligible to play.

Let me explain what being *academically ineligible* means. There are rules in college, set by the NCAA and/or your college, that set GPA cutoffs for academic eligibility. If you don't make them, you don't play. It's that simple. If you don't play, your value to the coach decreases, and you could lose your scholarship and could subsequently be dropped from the team.

It's a snowball effect. Once you have momentum it's hard to stop the snowball. It just keeps growing and growing. So, how do you develop this snowball of good grades and fortune? You develop good time-management skills and good test-taking skills. Here are some tips:

Time Management

- Devote a set amount of time, each day, to your studies, and stick to it.

- Write down all assignments (when you write it down, it makes it real).

- Take advantage of study hall time; get your work done during school, if at all possible, so you can go have fun after school.

- When you complete an assignment, cross it off. (It's a psychological thing; it will make you feel like you accomplished something, which you did! Yippee!)

- Organize your assignments, worst to best. If you start with your worst assignment, you will be stronger and more able to complete it. If you wait until the end of your study time to work on it, you will have no motivation to complete it. If you end on a good assignment, you will complete it with ease and you will begin to establish the pattern of completing all tasks.

- If it's a long-range assignment, work on it, just a little, each day. For example, if you have a month-long project, break it up into small parts, and then write down when and how you will do each part. By working on the project a little bit each day, it becomes much more manageable and you will complete it without rushing.

- Do not procrastinate! Get it done now and go have fun!

- Work with friends. There is a saying: "misery loves company." As long as you have to do an assignment (that is the misery part), why not enjoy the company of your friends? More than that, though, I believe that two or three heads full of knowledge beat one any day! If you develop a small group of friends you study with, and you don't spend too much time talking, you will get your work done that much faster. And if you have questions, your friends will be able to answer them faster than you can look up the answer.

Test-Taking Skills

Here are some techniques that help with all types of test taking:

- The most important thing is to go into each and every exam well prepared.

- Do your homework.

- Anticipate what is going to be on the exam and study that.

- Go over *memorizable* information over and over again.

- Quiz yourself, have your friends quiz you, and have your parents quiz you.

- Create test questions for yourself and your friends.

- Know the material frontward and backward.

- Make sure you are well rested for the exam.

- Don't forget to breathe for relaxation during the exam.

Multiple-choice exams

Multiple choice exams are created to lure you into choosing an answer prematurely, before you have had time to think it through. Here is a technique I teach to medical students and high school students to keep them from choosing an answer before some resemblance of a thought has occurred: For each question, cover up the answer choices, read the question, write down everything you know about it, and try to come up with an answer to the question before you uncover the choices. Once you have tried to answer the question, uncover each answer choice, one at a time, and follow the protocol below:

When you uncover "A," you must say: "Choice A is true because . . ." or "A is false because . . ." You must give a reason why it's true or false. If it's false, cross it off and move on. If you are not quite sure about it being true and you think it has merit and could be true, put a question mark next to the choice and move on. Do this with "B," "C," and "D."

Hopefully, if you have studied as much as you should have, you will be able to choose the correct answer without too much angst. If not, then do process of elimination. Cross out the answer choices you know for sure are incorrect, and then you will probably be left with two choices. Try to see if there is something within the wording that helps you tip the scale of one answer choice being either true or false.

Or, if you know that one part of the sentence is "false," then the entire statement becomes false.

For example: "Playing college soccer involves a lot of hard work and dedication, and you always get a lot of time for your studies."

There are two things in this sentence that should tip you off that it is incorrect: (1) as I have been saying, a great deal of your time is spent refining your soccer skill, traveling, practicing, and scrimmaging, leaving little time for studying. So, that third part of the sentence makes the entire sentence false, even though the first two parts are true. (2) The word "always" should be a huge clue. Be very careful when you see extreme words like "always" and "never."

The Assessment and Run Through

Prior to beginning the test, page through the entire test: how many pages, how many questions, are they long questions or short questions? Guesstimate how much time the test should take you. By not rushing into it right away, you bring a level of calm, an understanding of what is expected, and an assessment of how much time it will take to complete the exam. Once you begin the test, go though the entire test and answer only the questions that are easy for you, skipping ones that are harder and will take more time to think through.

On your second run through, begin to tackle the more difficult questions, always trying to narrow your choices to two, and then making an educated guess between the two. If time allows, go through the test one more time, back to front, making sure you have answered the questions correctly—making sure you didn't mark "B" when you meant "A"—this time the goal is to catch any silly errors.

The Rule for Changing Your Answer

Never, ever, ever change your answer unless you know *why* you are changing it. For example, if you meant to choose "B" and you accidentally marked "A," then that is a valid reason to change your answer. Or, if you realize your thinking was incorrect, or you found the correct answer in a question later in the test, that is okay, too. However, if you say, "Well, it could be 'C,' I guess I will change it," that is *not* a good reason to change it. Always go with your gut, what you originally chose, unless you have made a careless mistake or the information comes to you later in the test.

Essay

The key to an essay exam is to have already built an outline of what you would write. Usually, your teacher will give you the topics ahead of time and say, "Here are six questions I'm going to ask. I will choose three for you to write on." Develop six outlines, commit them to memory, and once you receive your test, use a sheet of paper to write out each of the outlines before you begin writing the essay.

Short answer

Use complete sentences and watch your penmanship. You want what you have written to count, so make it legible, be clear, and be concise.

Time

Regardless of the type of test—multiple choice, essay, short answer, fill in the blank, or matching—always be aware of your time. Only as a last resort, when time is running out, should you just randomly choose an answer; don't read the question, just choose. Even if you get the question wrong, you would have missed it if you hadn't answered it. If, however, by chance you get it correct, then that puts you ahead of the game.

Athletics

In addition to developing your academic skills, you must also continue to develop your soccer skills and make decisions, often difficult ones, which strategically put you in a position to advance your soccer career. This requires careful consideration of your club team, the Olympic Development Program, and your high school team. Additionally, whenever you travel with teams or go on vacations with your family, go on unofficial visits to universities and colleges.

Club Team

Without a doubt, one of the most important things you can do to increase your chances of playing college soccer is to play on a competitive club team. Playing on a premier or a regional traveling team typically implies a level of commitment and training beyond the norm. On competitive teams there is usually a licensed coach, trainers, or guest coaches that regularly teach skill and tactical development. There will also be more opportunities for travel to competitive tournaments where you will compete against other highly skilled players and gain exposure to college coaches.

Additionally, a team comprised of players who share the goal of playing college soccer has players who rarely miss practices, a commitment to a high level of fitness, a variety of trainers, supportive parents, and a coach with a strategic eye to advance all girls to collegiate play. When the majority of players on a team have a goal of playing in college, more can be accomplished because players are willing to push themselves and each other. Everyone develops, everyone works hard, and hopefully, everyone has fun.

However, if your club team decides to enter the regional league, you may have to choose between high school play and the regional league, as the seasons may overlap. I have created a list of positives and negatives for playing in high school versus playing the regional league for you to consider below.

This is where we get into a bit of a sticky wicket. I'm not really sure what a sticky wicket is, but I know it's a mess! There are positives and negatives to playing on your high school team. I will present them and let you make your own decisions.

Positives

- You have an opportunity to represent your high school.
- Your friends, teachers, and community will see you play.
- You will probably be the star of the team—something that is rarely felt in college.

- The coach will probably expect you to be a captain and leader. This is an excellent opportunity to develop your leadership skills for the rest of your life and a great thing to put on a résumé.
- You may win city and state titles, both personally and as a team.

Negatives

- Competition isn't usually as good as club or regional traveling teams.
- Exposure to college coaches is negligible.
- Skill level isn't as good as club or regional traveling teams.

Okay, I can't stand it; I need to share my opinion. I can't just present the pros and cons and leave it at that. Take my opinion for what it's worth. You are just a kid; be a kid. Enjoy high school; enjoy your friends and all that high school has to offer. There is no better feeling than representing your school and community. There will be plenty of time to grow up, be responsible, and make life-altering decisions. But for today, choose to be a kid and choose what makes you happy. I realize everyone must make their own decisions; just make sure you base yours on your heart!

Olympic Development Program (ODP)

If you are lucky enough to not live too far away from your state's ODP hub and you have given it a try and made the pool or state team, continue. As I talk about in the next chapter, ODP can give you increased exposure to college coaches, excellent training, skill and tactical development, and the mental toughness needed to play college soccer.

Sophomore Year

Academics

Your sophomore year is no different than your freshman year, with the exception that you have already developed good study skills and habits. Continue to refine and develop them and work toward achieving the grades you are capable of attaining.

One additional thing I suggest you do this year is take your school's career inventory (i.e., what you want to be when you grow up). This will assess your personality and help you determine what careers might be a good fit. I think these can be helpful; however, my daughter was told she should be a steamboat captain! She turned out to be a commercial airline pilot. I guess it's kind of close. Nonetheless, give it a try.

I also recommend shadowing people in the community who do something that interests you. Use your friends' parents as possible candidates to shadow, ask your parents for contacts, and ask your teachers and counselors for contacts. This is called networking; it always helps to know someone who knows someone who may know someone who could be helpful.

Also, start contacting colleges and universities for information about their school and programs. Be sure to review academic requirements for admissions.

Athletics

During your sophomore year, it is important to continue to play on the most competitive club team, and if you have chosen to play ODP, continue in this endeavor. After your sophomore year, during the summer, there are seven things you need to do:

- Take the Academic Questionnaire found in the chapter titled "Divisions I, II, and III: Three Levels, Three Lifestyles." This will help you identify what type of college experience you are looking for.
- Based on the results of the Academic Questionnaire, begin to identify schools that fit your criteria.
- Take the Soccer Survey in that same chapter. This will help you determine the degree to which you want soccer to play a part in your college experience and the commitment you are willing to make to playing in college, given your educational and career goals.
- Identify soccer programs using *Soccer America* and/or www.NCAA.org.
- Begin writing coaches for information about their programs and to express interest. Based on both my daughters' experiences, every coach they wrote responded very favorably to their inquiries.
  - Review all materials received by coaches, and if you have questions send a follow-up

letter, e-mail, or call. Remember, coaches are not allowed to initiate contact with you yet, so if you want to talk to them, you must contact them.

- If you do not have any questions, make a decision now: is it a potential school or not? Either way, file the information.
- Use family vacations and soccer travel to squeeze in some unofficial visits.

Junior Year

This is a very big year for both your academics and your athletics. There is a great deal to accomplish. It's important to stay organized, calm, and focused.

Academics

- Continue to do as well as possible in your classes and keep focusing on your time-management and test-taking skills.
- This is the year you will take one or both of the national college entrance exams, the SAT and ACT. Which exam you take depends on where you are applying to college. Most schools in the East use the SAT and schools in the Midwest to West use the ACT. Check first before taking them.
- Meet with your high school counselor to ensure you meet all college admissions requirements.

Athletics

- Play on the most competitive club team and participate in ODP.
- Continue to review materials received from colleges and coaches.
- Make a videotape of your play.
- Create a soccer résumé.
- Send coaches your itinerary of summer tournaments.
- Send your videotape and résumé in late spring.
- Go on unofficial visits.

*College coaches are allowed to make one phone call to you in March.

Summer after Junior Year

- Attend tournaments.
- Keep communicating with coaches. On July 1, coaches can begin to call you once a week. Be prepared!
- Register at the NCAA Clearinghouse online. DI and DII use the Clearinghouse. For DIII, contact the colleges for specific policies and financial aid.
- Retake ACT/SAT depending on your score.
- Continue unofficial visits to campuses and soccer programs.

Senior Year

This is a great year, filled with both excitement for what lies ahead of you and a bit of sadness as you prepare to say farewell to old friends and your childhood. You are pretty much an adult now. The decisions you make will impact your life forever.

Academics

- Continue to get good grades and refine your time-management and test-taking skills.
- Retake ACT/SAT, if needed.

Athletics

- Continue to play on the most competitive club team.
- Continue ODP.
- Schedule your official visits. They can start on the opening day of classes of your senior year. You have five official visits for DI and DII and unlimited for DIII.
- Continue to take unofficial visits.
- Continue to contact coaches and programs.
- February 1 is *National Signing Day* (the day you may sign a Letter of Intent to play for DI and DII when an athletic scholarship is involved).

Communication with coaches is now all verbal. Coaches are trying to get to know you as you should be trying to get to know them. By now, they have seen you play and are heavily into the recruiting process. Their goal is to get you to commit; your goal is to not commit until you are sure about the program and school *and* have negotiated the very best financial deal for yourself (see "Researching Soccer Programs, Attending Official Visits, and Negotiating the Scholarship: The Goal Is in Sight!").

Each coach will try to find a set time to call you each week. Given that the coaches have seen you play, you can now begin to talk about how you fit into the mix, your position(s), where they see you contributing, etc.

The "To Do" List

The following table summarizes your "To Do" list for each year of high school to prepare for a college soccer career. Once you have completed each step, simply place a checkmark next to the one in the table to indicate that you've completed it. Remember, preparing for a collegiate soccer career requires attention to completing each of the steps identified in the table and developing and refining your soccer abilities *and* academic skills.

To Do	Freshman	Sophomore	Junior	Senior
Play competitive club	✔	✔	✔	✔
Get good grades	✔	✔	✔	✔
Play ODP	✔	✔	✔	✔
Attend competitive tournaments	✔	✔	✔	✔
Take Soccer Survey		✔		
Take Academic Questionnaire		✔		
Take career interest inventories		✔	✔	
Research and contact schools and programs		✔	✔	✔
Review materials from programs and file accordingly		✔	✔	
Take ACT/SAT			✔	
Retake ACT/SAT			✔	✔
Write cover letter			✔	
Make video			✔	
Write résumé			✔	
Send coaches cover letter, résumé, game schedule, video			✔	
Go on unofficial visits	✔	✔	✔	✔
Go on official visits				✔
Register in NCAA Clearing house				✔

The Olympic Development Program

What's in It for Me?

ODP is an intense program, but don't take it too seriously. If your personal ODP goals are not met, it's not the end. There are numerous other ways to get noticed by college coaches. The most important thing to remember is *you* hold the key to your future. Hard work and determination are never overlooked.

Ashley Weimer, Defender,
West Virginia

Introduction

What I have learned about the Olympic Development Program (ODP) is that it varies from state to state with regard to organization, structure and intensity; everyone has an opinion about the program, its worth, what is gained from participating, the trainings, the pressure, the coaches, and the administrators. And no discussion about ODP is ever complete without stories of politics, favoritism, and scandal.

The young women who participated in my survey harbor pretty strong feelings about ODP, too. They either really liked it or they really hated it, with not much in between. Most players acknowledge the politics; some players said the politics ruined their experience, while others said that even with the politics, ODP was worthwhile.

In this chapter I hope to tease out the subtle and not-so-subtle nuances of ODP for you. It certainly took me more than a few years to figure out why it existed and how to use the program to promote a player's soccer career. For all that ODP is—good and bad—knowing how to use it to your advantage can be essential to your soccer development and emotional well-being. Heidi Westrum from St. Cloud State said it best:

> I feel I could have used my ODP experience as more of an advantage if I knew how to use it as one.

Well, Heidi, this is the crux of this chapter. In addition to figuring out how to take advantage of your ODP experience, this chapter will answer the following questions: What is ODP? How does it work? What are its strengths? What are its weaknesses? What do girls who have been through the program and have played soccer in college think of it? Is this a credential worth having and sacrificing for?

I also have included in this chapter a "golden nugget." It is something to think about when you or someone you know doesn't make ODP, a club, or college team. It is something that needs to be committed to memory and called upon before one's self-esteem as a soccer player is challenged.

*The following information on tryouts, pool teams, event teams, coaches, and camp is based on my experiences in the state of Wisconsin and within the region. How other states and regions conduct each of these milestones may differ. Based on what the players who completed my survey have disclosed about their experiences regarding the politics, the favoritism, and the overall structure of ODP, it appears to be similar across the states represented in my survey.

What is ODP?

I know this will come as a shock to you, but what I am about to tell you is something many people don't ever realize while they are involved in ODP: the state ODP program exists solely to pick a regional team. The regional team exists solely to pick a national team. Period! The goal of the Olympic Development Program is to identify talented players within each state and region who may have the potential to play on the national team. The national team exists to identify players for international play.

So, what happens to the rest of the players if they don't make the regional or national teams? They will have plenty of opportunities for exposure and development during camp. This will be covered in the section on camp.

How ODP Works

Developmental Program

The Olympic Development Program begins at U-13; players are eleven and twelve years old. It is an all-inclusive program that does not cut any players. Young players are exposed to ODP's coaching staff and structure. Training sessions and a developmental mini-camp are part of the experience. No state team is picked from this age group.

The Pool Team

At thirteen years of age (U-14), players are eligible to attend tryouts for the state's pool team. Fifty or more players are usually selected for pool training. Pool tryouts may be held at a central or a not-so-central location in a player's home state. All players are welcome to register for tryouts. Tryouts are held for each age division. Girls who have participated in ODP, who have made the state, regional, and national teams in previous years, continue to try out each year as well.

Over a series of training sessions, players are evaluated for the pool team. The coaches will mix up the players and their positions to see who works well together and who complements each other based on skill and talent. All of a sudden a player who has always been a forward may find herself playing defense as the coach develops a feel for where she can be most effective given the rest of the players and their abilities.

Coaches watch, train, and make notes on clipboards about players they are interested in watching. This is the beginning of the clipboards! At ODP camp, as a chaperone,

I always heard from the players about the dreaded clipboards carried by evaluators. We will talk about the significance of this later in the chapter.

Players are notified, usually by mail, if they made the "pool team." The state team will eventually be picked from the pool team.

> The first two years of ODP are a lot of pressure. I got used to it as I played more and more through the years, but it was rough on my confidence at times, always waiting to hear if you were cut or not. I put a lot of pressure on myself when I was younger and drove myself to the point of tears many times. But at the same time I always went back because I knew that it was going to get me where I wanted to go.
>
> *Anonymous,*
> *University of Massachusetts*

If a player makes the pool team, she will have practices to attend, hopefully in a central location in her state. It is common for some players to have to travel quite a distance for practice. I've known players who lived as many as four hours away and would wake up before dawn to come to a team practice. Now that is commitment!

In addition to training sessions, the pool teams often travel out of state to play in tournaments. Not every pool player may attend the event. Thus, an "event team" is picked from the state pool team.

I remember a very wise woman at ODP camp who would meet with players and give mini-seminars on career counseling once said, "If you don't like ODP, you won't like Division I." At the time, not knowing what Division I was like, I just filed the comment away. But after watching what my daughter went through at DI, I now realize how right she was.

Imagine: It's early spring; it's snowing, cold, and early in the morning. As a member of the state pool team, your thirteen-year-old daughter is eligible to try out for the event team that is traveling to San Diego for the Surf Cup tournament. As her parent, you have been instructed to bring an envelope with a check for the cost of the flight and your daughter's name on the outside.

The tryout lasts two very long hours. Parents are wrapped in blankets, standing on the sidelines shivering for themselves and for their daughters. The girls are wearing shorts or sweats, T-shirts, some with gloves, some without. Their little arms and legs are red and blue with cold. They are all playing their hearts out.

Every little girl wants to be picked to go to San Diego and play soccer. Every soccer mom and dad wants their daughter to be chosen and watches with a careful eye to see if the coach just saw what amazing thing their daughter just did.

The tryout ends. The coach gathers the girls and parents together and explains the procedure for notification. He collects the envelopes from the girls and tells them to go wait in their cars and vans, warm up, and he will take approximately twenty minutes to sort out paperwork and pick the team. He explains to the girls that he will hand back their envelope. If they made the team, there will be an itinerary in place of the check in the envelope. If they did not make the team, their check will still be in the envelope.

He further instructs them that they are not to open their envelopes until they get back into their vehicles and have left the premises.

Once back in your vehicle, your first priority is helping your daughter out of her cold, snow-soaked clothes. Your second priority is to try to pass those agonizing twenty minutes with talk about anything but soccer, so the conversation is light and the snacks are plenty.

Finally, after what seems like an eternity, the coach emerges from his car with the envelopes. Everyone gathers around him as he reiterates the rules: "no opening the envelope until you have left the premises." Like nothing you have ever experienced before, in a matter of minutes, mass chaos ensues. The girls try not to open their envelopes but the temptation is just too great, the stakes are much too high. The school parking lot, in a matter of minutes, fills with laughter, tears, hugs, and consoling. As you walk off with your daughter you can't help but wonder what your daughter has gotten into.

The coaches who are chosen to participate in ODP may also be a high school coach, a club coach, a college player, an ex-college player, an ex-professional player, or a college coach. All have been chosen based on their reputation in the state. I believe the coaches are all "A" licensed (the highest level). Some say they are chosen for political reasons; I cannot confirm or deny that statement. Most of the coaches in my state appeared to be competent, compassionate, and interested in bettering the players in their charge.

The State Team and Camp

Throughout the year, the pool team will attend a variety of training sessions. They may scrimmage other in-state and out-of-state teams, either younger or older, and attend tournaments where an event team must be picked to represent the state. In the spring, the state team is picked. For the younger teams, two teams (thirty-six players) may be chosen to represent the state. For the older players, one team (eighteen players) is chosen. Once the team is picked, the players begin to refine their skills and scrimmage other teams in preparation for the ODP camp.

Camp is hard emotionally and psychologically. Physically, the camp is not too tough. Players have team trainings a couple of times a day and compete against other teams in their region. In this endeavor, they are continuously evaluated for the next level of play. There are also lectures that cover nutrition, sports psychology, and collegiate play.

While players are practicing and competing, coaches ride around in golf carts, with the dreaded clipboards, trying to identify players who fit their ideal. A player's state coach can also make recommendations to the regional team coach regarding which player should be given a pool tryout. At the end of each day, players are sorted into "A" pool, "B" pool and the "remaining" players.

"A" pool is the highest group, and these players are being considered for the regional pool team. "B" pool players show some promise; they will be watched closely. If a player is invited to join either "A" or "B" pool trainings, she will train the next morning with the prospective pool team instead of her state team.

Players will move throughout the week between "A" and "B" pools and their regular state team depending on how their training sessions progress. At a moment's notice, without a word of explanation, a player may slip from the "A" pool all the way back down to the state team training.

Using ODP to Your Advantage

So what about the players who didn't get picked for the "A" and "B" pools? I used to think they were just appeased through daily trainings and lectures. And that can seem like a fact to a young girl who has played her heart out and still not made a pool the entire camp. With the knowledge that the only reason the state team exists is to pick the regional team, one can feel like a cast off. But don't!

Herein lies what Heidi from St. Cloud was talking about at the beginning of the chapter: if you don't make it to the "A" or "B" pool, then you should use your ODP state team position to your advantage. Taking advantage of the ODP experience can often be clouded by emotions. Because of the psychological implications associated with not getting picked for the "A" or "B" pools, you may want to just give up. You may begin to doubt your soccer prowess, your ability to play college soccer, and your self-esteem as a player.

ODP camp has a way of making girls feel totally inadequate. This is the mental aspect of ODP. This is where you will learn if you have mental toughness—the ability to get kicked around emotionally and come back each day fighting with an attitude that says: "I know I am good, I know I possess great skills and ability, you can't shake my confidence. I know who I am as a player and I am happy with that." Mental toughness is another dimension many DI coaches value.

You must learn to use ODP just as much as ODP is using you. There are four key ways to use ODP camp to your advantage. First, soak in all the feedback coaches are providing. Use all the training sessions to refine your skills and emerge from camp a better player.

The second way to take advantage of ODP camp is to work hard, show up prepared to give 110% effort, and stay positive. Why? Because college coaches are at camp with clipboards, riding around in golf carts watching you!

Remember, it's only natural that college coaches who participate in ODP have a dual purpose for working the camp. I'm sure their personal motivations for participating are numerous, but their professional role as a college coach always ensures an eye on identifying a potential recruit. Coaches are looking for the girl who is always hustling, who gives her all, who is positive, and who can make a contribution to the team. Coaches don't want a player if all she does is whine and exhibits a bad attitude. If you bring your best to the field each day, you will increase your chances of being noticed and eventually recruited!

Yes, it would be nice to make the "A" or "B" pool, but if it doesn't happen, then take advantage of the captive audience: the coaches. They are still there training you! They still have their clipboards. Believe me; they are always in the recruiting mode. Their jobs depend on it.

The third way to take advantage of an ODP experience is to use the credential. If you make it to the pool team or above, you now have an ODP credential to put on your résumé, which can set you apart from other players. When a college coach looks at your résumé with an ODP credential and then compares it to a player who doesn't have an ODP credential, if the coach has to make a decision regarding who to go see, more times than not, the coach will choose you, the player with ODP experience.

> Playing ODP gives the recruit the edge over the other players that have never played ODP. College coaches seem to like to see the letters ODP.
>
> *Anonymous,*
> *University of West Florida*

The fourth way to use ODP to your advantage is the travel. If you make the pool team or above, you may have opportunities to travel. You may travel across your state or to warm, sunny places out of state. (What can I say, I'm from Wisconsin; traveling to San Diego in November was heaven.) Although the travel and excitement can often be more than enough experience, meeting and competing against new players is an opportunity to make friends and can give you the chance to compare yourself to other players. Your perception of yourself as a player may change as you compete against other talented players. An honest appraisal of your abilities and talents can facilitate your personal growth and development.

So, is it the end of a dream to play college soccer if you don't make ODP? No! If you do not make ODP or choose not to participate, for whatever reason, all hope is not lost of playing college soccer. Here are some compelling quotes to think about from the girls who participated in my survey:

> Everyone told me that you needed to play ODP if you wanted to get recruited, well that just isn't true! Different states may be different, but if it was run anything like mine was, ODP was only a waste of time. What really mattered was your club team and getting your name out to college coaches.
>
> *Erica Baker, Defense,*
> *Western Kentucky*

I think it is good to try out and see what it is like. It is not for everyone. I went to a great school where some played ODP and some did not. You don't have to play ODP to play soccer in college. I do believe though, that DI coaches do look more closely at that.

Anonymous,
University of Indianapolis

ODP helped me develop my skills by playing against a higher level of competition. ODP focused on making each player better, and I think it helped.

Nicky Snyder,
Barton College

Try it. It may be difficult because of its competitive nature. It can be brutally honest. But don't let it deter your dreams of becoming a collegiate athlete. Take the experience and learn from it.

Amy Holst, Midfield,
Ball State

A Golden Nugget

And here is probably the biggest golden nugget in this entire book that applies to ODP as well as the entire recruiting process:

Whatever a coach values, whether it is a skill, a style, or a behavior, if you do not possess it, you probably will not be recruited by that coach. It is nothing personal; it's just human nature to recruit players who fit into one's ideal.

I think it is important to read this over as many times as needed until it sinks in. Dog ear this page and come back to it until it becomes a tape in your head. It will save you tons of wondering, tons of self-doubt, and tons of anguish.

For example, watch a college team play. Look at each one of the players. Can you figure out what that coach values? I remember watching the Illinois women's soccer team play a few years ago and noticing the players were all short, very muscular, and fast. A tall, lean, and not-so-fast player was not to be had.

A player may have ten *other* great qualities, but if she doesn't have the one thing the coach values, that one thing the coach always looks for in a player, the coach may not value what she brings to the field.

And just because a player may not have that one thing doesn't mean she won't ever make it to the next level of ODP or a college team. It only means the player hasn't found her match yet. She hasn't found the coach who happens to value that one thing she brings to the field.

Okay, so you may be thinking: if a player has ten fantastic things but lacks the one thing a coach values, she won't get recruited by them? The answer is probably yes. It's really not personal. It's all about that one thing.

So what should you do? Always stay positive, show off your individual abilities, and always come ready to play. Don't forget, there are a lot of coaches doing team trainings, and there might be a couple of these coaches who value what you bring to the soccer field. You should show them your skills and talents, your heart, your drive, your determination, and your spirit.

To summarize the strengths and weaknesses of ODP, I have provided a list below:

Strengths of ODP in a Nutshell

- A credential to put on your soccer résumé
- Travel within-and out-of-state
- Exposure to college coaches
- Excellent training (depending upon the state)
- Meet other players from different states
- Develop your mental game
- Compare your skills and abilities to other players'

Weaknesses of ODP in a Nutshell

- A lot of pressure
- Political
- May not capture the best in state if tryouts/ trainings are held too far away from some players' homes
- Some states don't have a well-developed program

Is ODP Worthwhile?

To determine ODP's worthwhileness, we can look to the player responses to six questions. The first four questions were open-ended and the final two questions provide statistical data.

For the first question, "How did ODP help you?" I was able to categorize the players' comments into four areas: personal improvement, the credential, exposure, and personal revelation.

Personal Improvement

Within this category players mentioned improving their skills, technical, tactical, and ball; learning to adapt their play to align with different coaches and teammates; using evaluations and feedback to raise their own personal bar; learning to play with other females and to play women's-style soccer (some girls had only played on boys' teams); and learning to see how important it was to increase their commitment to achieving their goals.

> Playing ODP, you have to learn to adapt to the players around you and to the different styles of play. It is a great learning experience.
>
> *Joni Vickers, Forward/Midfield,*
> *University of Georgia*

The Credential

The second area, the credential, was just that. Players talked about ODP being a résumé booster.

Exposure

Within the third area, exposure, players mentioned two types of exposure: traveling to tournaments and meeting college coaches. Both were mentioned very favorably. Playing with other players encouraged players to compare their abilities and talents to other players and evaluate their soccer goals in comparison to other players. Exposure to a variety of coaches allowed players to market themselves to a broad audience and also learn what it's like to be valued in terms of what you can do for a coach. Many players said this helped them prepare for DI.

Personal Revelation

The next area, personal revelation, is where players talked about commitment and motivation. Because players are told ODP is like DI, many players said their experience at ODP solidified their desire to *not* play DI. Most players commented negatively on the time obligation, stating that they did not want soccer to be their life. Consequently, these players chose to play at DII and DIII schools. Additionally, some players talked about how their ODP experience decreased their motivation to play soccer in general. These players realized they wanted to do other things with their time, such as participate in a second sport.

The second open-ended question I asked players was, "What did you like most about ODP?" I categorized responses into six groups: challenge, skill development, competition, exposure, social, and nothing.

Challenge

In this category players talked about ODP being both a physical and mental challenge. The mental challenge or mental toughness refers to the ability to keep one's head up through adversity. Playing one's very best game only to find out it wasn't good enough to make the cut and then coming back the next day for more is mental toughness. Dealing with the politics, the stress of constant evaluation, and even dealing with the cliques exemplifies mental toughness.

The mental toughness required to play ODP is something to be admired. I don't know if players are just born with it or can learn it; I only know it is a much greater challenge than the physical aspects of ODP. The following quote says a great deal, given its simplicity:

Start early with ODP and play for as long as you can stand it.

Anonymous,
Clemson University

This player's comment captures the mental toughness a player must have to stay with ODP. I sincerely applaud every player who has played ODP.

Physical

The physical challenge players talked about primarily deals with being out of one's comfort zone, learning new styles of play, learning to play a new position, and the physicality of play and the drills.

Skill Development

Most players highlighted learning new skills, both technical and tactical. Some players also mentioned the work ethic they developed playing at this level.

ODP provided me with an amazing opportunity to grow as an athlete and a person. I became the soccer player I was in college with the skills and coaching I learned from ODP.

Anonymous,
University of North Carolina-Pembroke

Competition

Players were able to identify players on their own team and on opposing teams that they viewed as better players and who challenged them to step up their own personal game. This type of personal competition was viewed as ideal for development.

Exposure

Most player responses centered on the importance of putting oneself out there—the marketing of one's skills and talents. Players believed that the tournaments they traveled to, along with the many coaches they encountered at the regional camps, were ideal for gaining the necessary exposure for recruiting.

Social

It was nice to see that many players talked about the positive aspects of meeting and playing new players. It is not all cliques. In fact, many players reported that the players they met through ODP were also the players they encountered playing with or against in college. It was positively reported that they enjoyed developing this social network.

Some players who attended the regional camp became very clear that they wanted a life that included soccer, but not soccer *as life*. This is an important distinction to think about as many DI programs require the type of commitment that requires soccer *is life*.

> I had the opportunity to meet other amazing soccer players and friends with my same goals and aspirations.
>
> *Anonymous,*
> *University of North Carolina-Pembroke*

The third open-ended question I asked players was: "What did you like least about ODP?" and I categorized the responses into six categories: cliques, competition, coaches, politics, time, and everything else I lumped into "other."

Cliques

A number of players across all divisions talked about the cliques in ODP. Some players seemed to think the ODP teams were comprised of one or two club teams in the state and only a very small number of players from different teams. It would appear that the familiarity of players in combination with the competitiveness of ODP creates a cliquey climate as players commented about the girls being "mean," "snotty," "having an attitude," and being "deceitful."

> Players would hog the ball and not pass to certain players to show off themselves and their friends.
>
> *Anonymous,*
> *University of Arkansas*

> Most of the state pool was made up of girls from one club team and I was not a member of that club. Therefore, I felt like an outcast most of the time.
>
> *Sara Murray, Forward,*
> *Truman State University*

Competition

A lot of players talked about the competition in ODP being overwhelming. There is the constant stress of not making the cut, feeling anxious about the mistakes you made on the field, and the lack of team unity because everyone is out for herself. As I have said before, many believe that if you don't like the competition in ODP, you won't like DI.

Coaches

The responses about cliques felt by many players about their fellow teammates were reiterated regarding coaches. Players commented on coaches being "mean," "cliquey," and having favorites. Players also wrote about coaches being demeaning, not trying to get to know the players personally, and promoting players from the coach's own club team.

Politics

> Many people say ODP is political, and it is! But isn't everything political in life? I think some decisions are made just because of connections and not always about talent seen from players on the field. In addition, I think that each time you reach a higher level it's that much harder to break on to the team because of coaches not knowing who you are. If you are a new girl on the regional pool, it's harder for you to make the team because the majority of the rest of the players have been on it since the beginning.
>
> *Anonymous,*
> *Penn State*

Whenever one mentions the word "ODP," the next comment inevitably has to do with the politics. I have heard outlandish stories of parents buying cars for coaches or sending coaches on trips with the promise of promoting their daughter. Are they true? I have no clue!

All I really do know is most everyone believes ODP is political. And, it is this political aspect that causes an overwhelming amount of angst among parents and players.

Under the watchful eye of parents, players are picked who don't seem to have the talent, speed, or skills that their daughter does. It is often baffling why some players are promoted and others are not. Is it because a player's mom or dad is someone important in ODP or the state? Is it because the coach, who is also a college coach, has some sort of agenda? Or is it simply because of that one thing a coach wants, like we talked about earlier?

In addition to the overwhelming comments about the politics in ODP, players reported that the younger they started ODP the better because older players trying out for the first time may not be given a chance to play. Players also talked about the importance of being from the right club team or being "shoe-ins" because they had always been on the team.

> I think ODP is very political. Being from a small state, we never really got noticed and we were the joke of camp. No one really ever got much out of ODP from my state, female-wise at least.
>
> *Audie Beckman, Forward,*
> *University of South Carolina–Aiken*

Politics, politics, politics. It you knew someone, you were in. I did not like that at all. It should be based on talent, but it is not.

Anonymous,
University of Indianapolis

There were times when someone would make the team just because they did the year before and their parents had a lot of influence over the staff.

Nicky Snyder,
Barton College

Very, very, very political. I have seen a lot of players who deserve to be on the regional team not make it and players who probably should have just made the state team make the regional team. There is a goalie that was on my club team and who now plays for the same college team that I do. Every year she would get shafted and not make the regional team. She played one year of college soccer and got spotted by a national team coach and is now playing for the U-20 national team. And believe me, I have played with this girl for over five years and she didn't make any huge leaps in her soccer ability.

Beth, Midfield/Defense,
Iowa State University

Time

Aside from it being political, the other recurring comment one usually hears associated with ODP is that it is time-intensive. Many players wrote about the travel to and from practice, having their weekends eaten up by practice and travel, the constant soccer, and the lack of any type of break from soccer.

Other

All other comments I lumped into this category. This category is comprised of comments relating to the expense of ODP, the level of disorganization, and the biggy: "everything." Many players commented that what they liked least about ODP was everything.

The fourth and final open-ended question was, "What advice would you give a player about ODP?" Players talked about the importance of challenging yourself. There are many challenges in ODP and the players I surveyed wanted future players to understand that the effort put into ODP is worth it even if you don't make it. By putting yourself out there for criticism and for comparison to other players in the state creates an opportunity for personal growth.

Players also said that it wasn't necessarily a bad thing if you try out for ODP and don't like it. In fact, an overwhelming number of players surveyed said, "Quit if you don't like it." They also said to be confident during tryouts, go into it with an open mind, and take it seriously, as this is the beginning of developing the mental toughness needed to play college soccer.

Another important point many players made was to start young. It appears that players believe it's harder to break into ODP the older you are.

Start as *early* as possible. The longer you are in the program, the better off you will be. The earlier you can get your name known to coaches, the better, because they will be looking for you as you grow up with the program. It's hard to come into ODP and get to know everyone the older you get.

Joni Vickers, Forward/Midfield,
University of Georgia

The final questions about ODP were: "How long did you play ODP and at what level?" They were included to provide data on the players surveyed. Additionally, these final questions address the question of ODP's worthwhileness, especially for DII and DIII.

In looking at the chart below, entitled "Number of Years Played," there are a couple of things worth noting. One, more than half of the players who responded to my survey in DII and DIII did not play ODP at all. In fact, if you look at the DIII column, you will notice that 24% of players played ODP for one year and then quit. I think that tells us something about ODP not being a necessity in order to play college soccer.

It's also interesting to note that one-third of the DI players did not participate in ODP. Again, a message that it may not be necessary. Moreover, for DI, if we look at the next highest percentage, after zero years played, we see that 26% of players played for five years. This tells us they were getting something positive out of it; otherwise, why would they have stayed so long?

Similarly, we see the same thing for DII players; the second largest percentage after zero year's played is four years. This does not hold true for DIII, as the second largest percentage is 24% and that is for one year of play.

By looking at the data, I think I can say with a reasonable amount of certainty that out of the girls who eventually played DI and DII, most found ODP to be a reasonably worthwhile program.

Years Played ODP	DI	DII	DIII
0	33%	63%	57%
1	4%	0%	24%
2	11%	8%	11%
3	18%	11%	6%
4	8%	12%	2%
5	26%	6%	0%

The sixth and final question I asked was, "What was the highest level of ODP you achieved?" The data in the chart below indicates that the highest level played across all divisions is the state team.

Additionally, if you look at the table above, under DI, you will see the highest percentage of players played for five years and the highest percentage of the players in DII played for four years. Given the longevity of play, it would appear that players felt they were gaining something by playing ODP.

The interesting thing about the data for DIII is that this group had the highest percentage of players who played on the state team, but the highest percentage of players who only played one year. The fact that these players only played for one year may indicate they either were not getting enough benefit from participating, they chose to spend their time elsewhere, or they may not have been asked back the following year.

Highest Level Played	DI	DII	DIII
State Pool	8%	26%	30%
State Team	36%	41%	43%
Regional Pool	23%	30%	23%
Regional Team	26%	3%	4%
National Pool	7%	0%	0%

It's not everything. Just because you don't make ODP doesn't mean you are not going anywhere. Just because you don't do ODP doesn't mean you are not good. I only did it one year because I had other sports commitments and that was in the end the best thing for me. I wouldn't trade the skills and memories I have in the other sports for spending more time at ODP. I am in college playing at a great and successful DII program and loving it. ODP will not make or break you.

Kathryn Kramer, Goalkeeper,
Winona State University

⚽ *To the Future Collegiate Player*

Is ODP worthwhile? Is it a credential worth sacrificing for? Is it worth not going to a high school dance because you have to travel that weekend with the team? Is it worth the emotional rollercoaster of whether or not you make the cut? Is it worth the tears as you find and develop the mental part of your game? Is it worth the criticism? The time? The effort? I think only you can answer these questions for yourself.

If you do decide to play ODP, keep in mind that it is easy to get completely wrapped up in who is making what team and who is wearing the "wild-colored jersey just to get noticed." This level of competition brings out not only one's aggressive nature, but a level of insanity not ever seen or experienced before. It's like your entire world rests on making it to the pool team, then to the state team, then to an "A" or "B" pool, then to the regional pool, and so forth.

Players I surveyed wanted you to know not to let it control your life, to relax, to try to have fun, to not get frustrated, and to understand that it's not the end of the world if you don't make it.

Hopefully knowing what you now know will allow you and your parents to keep it in perspective. If you decide to play ODP, no matter how long, use it to your advantage. Anticipate the myriad of feelings and emotions that come with ODP and glean everything you can from it for as long as you decide to participate.

 To the Parent of a Future Collegiate Player

As parents, it's important to provide an environment rich with love, support, and respect as your daughter enters the world of ODP. Always applaud her determination and decision-making and encourage her to make changes when necessary.

Letters, Résumés, Videotapes, and Communications

How to Stay in the Game

Introduction

Whether it's your cover letter or résumé, videotape or a phone conversation with a prospective coach, how and what you communicate is essential to your recruiting success. Each mode of communication is an opportunity to showcase your talents both on and off the field, as well as your intentions, motivations, and interests. It is your chance to tell the coach how and what you can contribute to his or her school's success; in other words, it's your chance to tell why they should recruit you.

In this chapter you will learn how to write a cover letter that grabs the coach's attention, a résumé that showcases all your relevant information, the importance of presentation and style, and how to create a videotape, what it should include, and its length. Statistics from the player surveys will be presented on how many collegiate players created résumés and videotapes within each division.

There are three adjectives to think about as you begin to develop your communication materials: *truthful, respectful,* and *professional.* Let's start with *truthful.* If you always make an effort to tell the truth, you won't be embarrassed if a coach questions you about what you said or wrote. I know it may seem tempting and harmless to add a couple of goals to your record or expound on your role in winning the state championship; however, if it's not the truth and the coach checks, your ever-so-slight exaggeration may become somewhat embarrassing. Be proud of who you are and what you have accomplished, and resist the urge to embellish.

Number two, be *respectful.* This means to mind your manners, just like your parents have probably told you before. Manners aren't just placing your napkin in your lap or chewing with your mouth closed; manners are your tone of voice, your attitude, and your choice of words. Your tone of voice and attitude can convey an entire array of characteristics about you. Manners can convey such things as whether you are pleasant or snotty, kind or mean, forthright or guarded, or goodhearted or selfish. Yes, you may think you are the next Mia Hamm or Briana Scurry and therefore believe every team would be lucky to have you, but keep that thought to yourself. Remember, the coach may be talking to twenty players at the same time he or she is talking to you. If all things are equal between you and another player, your attitude and tone of voice may be the deciding factor for the coach.

As for words, I am mainly talking about how you convey respect to each coach. For example, try to call the coach by her or his last name preceded by her or his title, which is coach. So if the coach's name is Mary Cleats, call her Coach Cleats. Avoid simply calling her Coach or by her first name, Mary. Think of each coach as a potential boss. Remember,

154

soccer is a business—you are the commodity and the coach may soon be your boss.

And the third area, *professional,* is sometimes easier to identify when someone isn't rather than when someone is. Fundamentally, it's having an articulate cover letter, a well-organized and visually appealing résumé, a high-quality videotape, and verbal communication that is forthright and responsive. This even applies when you contact coaches and they ignore you!

As a chaperone at ODP camp, I spent a lot of time talking to other soccer moms about their daughters, the team's successes each day, and what programs their daughters were going to apply to for college. One day, in between sticking cute, motivational messages and candy on our girls' dorm room doors and doing laundry, I ran into an upset mom. When I asked her what was wrong, she told me this story.

Her daughter's dream was to play soccer for one particular school. In her junior year the daughter sent the coach a letter and her résumé. When she didn't hear from the coach, she e-mailed him. When the coach didn't return her e-mails, she called. After waiting a couple of weeks, she tried calling and e-mailing him again. She had been repeating this cycle for the past few months. Mom had been watching her daughter agonize over the coach's lack of response and felt completely helpless in providing any wisdom.

As I listened to this mom, I wondered what was so hard about answering an e-mail or returning a phone call. How hard is it to afford someone such a simple courtesy? As I walked away and thought about what had happened to this player, I realized the coach had indeed communicated to her.

By taking a step back from this situation and taking out the emotion, the following can be inferred: for whatever reason, the coach was not interested in the player. The non-communication was sending the "not interested" message to this player.

Now, although this is not the most ideal way to conduct one's business, it happens. In fact, it will most likely happen to you! Coaches (and people in general), normally don't like to confront or hurt someone deliberately, so they hide behind silence. Imagine how hard it would be to say to a sixteen-year-old girl, "You know, when I look for a forward, I'm looking for these three traits, and you don't have them. Thank you for your interest in our program and good luck." It would be clear, honest, respectful, and professional, but it doesn't feel good, and that's why people avoid it.

What you always need to keep in mind is that it is not personal, it's business.

When a coach does not respond to you, do the following:

- Make three attempts to contact the coach.

- If you don't hear from the coach, repeat out loud to yourself: "It's not personal, it's business. I am a good player; I simply do not possess the particular traits the coach is looking for at this time."

- Move on.

Your Cover Letter

Your cover letter serves as a vehicle to deliver your résumé. It announces your résumé's arrival and your intentions and interests. The cover letter's role is just as important as the résumé and requires just as much thought.

Your cover letter will probably be the very first contact you will have with prospective coaches. You will need to include the following information: an appropriate salutation, your name, your objective for writing, why you are interested in this particular school, what you can contribute or what you have to offer that stands out from other players, and information about the enclosed résumé and game schedule.

Salutation

Each letter should be personalized; do not write "Dear Coach"; instead, write, "Dear Coach Cleats," using her or his last name only. Do not use the coach's first name. He or she deserves your respect.

Make sure the coach you are addressing is still there. You can do this by going on the school's website. There is nothing worse than receiving a letter addressed to someone else!

Objective

What is your purpose for writing this coach? State this clearly, concisely, and early. This is usually just a one-liner.

Suggestion:

- I am writing to you to express my interest in becoming a member of the Just for Kicks University soccer team.

Why You Are Interested in
Just for Kicks University

You want to show that you have done your research and know something particular about this school and program. Why you are interested should be genuine, not fictitious. Put some thought into this. You will set yourself apart from the competition by writing a personalized letter, as some of your peers may just write a generic letter.

Suggestions:

- I'd like to be a member of your team so that I can:
  - continue the winning tradition at Just for Kicks University.
  - play for a top-tier MAC team.
  - contribute to the rebuilding of Just for Kicks University program (if the program has been through a poor season recently or lost all their seniors).

What You Can Contribute to
Just for Kicks University

This is where you begin to sell yourself. If you have done your research and know the strengths and weaknesses of the program, you can tailor your comments accordingly. A coach may recognize insincerity, so try to write something that is an honest statement.

Suggestions:

- Your senior midfielders are all graduating, and I am a strong midfielder.
- I can add depth to your lineup.
- I can make an immediate impact to the defense.

What You Have Enclosed

The entire reason for writing this cover letter is to submit your résumé, game schedule, and videotape for review. Now is the time to tell the coach that you have included it.

Suggestions:

- I have enclosed my résumé for your review.
- I have also enclosed my game schedules for high school, club, and ODP for your convenience, along with a videotape of highlights.

Closing Statement

You always want to end the letter with a closing statement—something that conveys respect and an appreciation of the coach's time.

Suggestions:

- I greatly appreciate your time and consideration.
- I look forward to hearing from you.
- Thank you for your time.

Complimentary Closing

A complimentary closing precedes your signature. It conveys the closing of the letter and respect.

Suggestions:

- Sincerely
- Regards
- Respectfully

Signature

The signature section has four important components: your name, your signature, your position, and your number. The order is as follows:

- Your signature (neatness counts!)
- Your name, typed
- Your position, typed
- Your number, typed

The following is an example of a letter:

May 18, 2008

Coach Mary Cleats
Just for Kicks University
1517 Soccer Lane
Cleveland, OH 97245

Dear Coach Cleats,

I am writing to you to express my interest in becoming a member of the Just for Kicks University soccer team. My interest stems from my desire to play for a top-tier Mid-American Conference team.

In reviewing your statistics and current roster, I noticed all your key defenders are seniors and will be graduating this year. As a solid defender, I believe I can make an immediate impact and contribute to the Just for Kicks winning tradition.

I have enclosed a five-minute videotape of my game highlights for your review. I have also included my soccer résumé and game schedules for high school, ODP, and my club team.

I appreciate your time and consideration and look forward to hearing from you.

Sincerely,

Cindy Soccer

Cindy Soccer
Defender, #13

Résumé

In many cases your cover letter and résumé are your initial contact with college coaches. A clear, well-thought-out résumé and cover letter provide information to the coach that will put you into the *yes* pile, meaning he or she may come watch a game of yours, rather than the *no* pile, meaning you probably won't hear from that coach.

Your résumé is a statement about who you are both academically and athletically. It is your opportunity to draw attention to why you are worth considering, worth looking at, and most importantly, worth recruiting. It is your opportunity to put on paper what you have accomplished in the classroom, in your community, and on the field over the last four to five years.

What you say is just as important as how you say it and how it is presented. A good, comprehensive résumé should include all contact information, schools attended, your academic record, extracurricular activities, all soccer credentials and accomplishments, personal interests, and references.

Contact Information

You want to provide each coach every opportunity to contact you by giving him or her all of your contact information. You should include your:

- Name
- Address
- Phone number
- E-mail address
- Cell phone number

Schools Attended

List all high schools attended. Provide information on name, city, and state.

Academic Record

I cannot stress enough the importance of your academic record! It will open far more doors for you than anything else. If a coach sees that your grades are poor, she or he may choose another player to recruit. Coaches do not want to spend their time begging the admissions department on your behalf.

Moreover, if you lack concern for your academic record in high school, this may send a strong signal to the coach that a similar trend may follow in college. If your grades are poor in college, you may be placed on probation and ineligible to play soccer. At this point, you are no good to the coach. Remember, you are a commodity. Your worth is measured in your ability to perform.

A good academic record shows potential coaches that you are focused on achievement, are more than just a soccer player, and are someone who will always be academically eligible to play.

Additionally, if your grades are good, there will be more money for you in the realm of academic scholarships. These are scholarships based on GPA and/or SAT/ACT scores. Many coaches use both academic and athletic scholarships to recruit players.

What to include in the section on academic record:

- High school GPA to date
- Projected graduation GPA (If you're close enough to graduation to make an educated guess)

- SAT and/or ACT scores
- Scholastic awards and honors
- AP courses taken

Extracurricular Activities

Here is another opportunity to show you are well-rounded and focused beyond yourself. In this section you should include such things as:

- Volunteer experiences
- Other sports involvement
- Music/theater participation
- Community service through church/synagogue/ mosque or school

Soccer Credentials

Be honest, be accurate, and do not embellish!

- Soccer teams
- Club
- High school
- ODP
- Awards and honors
- Statistics:
  - Forward–goals and assists
  - Midfielder–goals and assists
  - Defender–shut-outs, goals, and assists
  - Goalie–shut-outs, goals against average

- Stature:
  - Height
  - Weight

You may be asking yourself why you should include information about stature. Sometimes coaches recruit players based on such things as stature, positions, aggressiveness, finesse, etc. Sometimes you will see almost an entire team of short and stocky players or tall and lean players; sometimes you will see the majority of a team that lacks finesse but possesses great aggressiveness. When these traits stick out on a team, it suggests the coach consistently recruits a certain type of player. To keep from wasting the coach's time and yours, put it on your résumé.

Personal Interests

Personal interests are the things you like to do when you have free time. Examples include:

- Reading
- Playing the piano
- Golf

References

Your choice of references is essential to your résumé, as they provide the prospective coach with an opportunity to find out some important information about you not found in your cover letter or résumé. This could be information such as whether you are easy to coach, a team player, a leader or a follower, internally motivated to excel or externally motivated by threats, a hard worker or a lazy player, and fit or out of shape.

In many cases, the prospective coach will contact someone they know who may know your reference. Thus, the information they gather may be second- or third-hand. So always keep in mind that your reputation precedes you; keep it first class.

Whom to include as a reference:

- Current or past club or high school coaches.
- Coaches with whom you attended camps.
- ODP coaches.
- Someone you know who plays/played for the coach.

Whom *not* to include as a reference:

- Your parents.
- Your friends.

Presentation

How you display your résumé and cover letter is an integral part of the package you submit to each coach. You will need to consider the following as you put the final touches on your résumé: layout, paper, font, and creativity.

Layout

How you choose to layout your résumé determines its visual appeal. The more appealing your résumé, the more time a coach will spend with it. Don't rush this process; it takes time and lots of revisions, and don't forget to have multiple people review it. Often, differing perspectives can provide valuable insight. Things to consider are:

- Line spacing; don't cram everything too close together.
- Clutter; keep it clear and simple.
- Keep it on one page.
- Headings should be bold.
- Subheadings; they may be underlined.
- Readability; it should be easy to read.
- Cleanliness, without smudges
- No misspellings
- No grammatical errors

Paper

For those of us who are tactile-sensitive, a nice-feeling paper is a good touch—pun intended! Go out and feel paper. Do you like smooth or bumpy, thick or thin? Once you have chosen paper type, think about color. White, shades of gray or tan, or a soft color that complements the school's colors can be good. Stay away from bright colors; they often make it hard to read. Remember, we want this to be a pleasant reading experience for the coach.

Font

Some fonts are harder to read than others. Play with this. Stay away from fonts that **cram** letters together or are *cursive*. Also, make sure you use at least a twelve-point font; anything smaller is hard to read. You can use bigger font for your **headings**.

Creativity

Do not be afraid to be creative in an effort to put your personal touch on the résumé and cover letter. For example, you could think about bolding your name in the color of the school or embellishing a picture of yourself in the upper right-hand corner; let your creative side come out. Just remember to be tasteful and do not go overboard. Also, think about coordinating both the résumé and cover letter, so that whatever you do to one, you do to the other.

I asked the players whether or not they created a résumé and found an overwhelming percentage took the time and effort to create a résumé across both DI and DII. For the players who chose DIII, a little more than half created a résumé.

The question then becomes whether you should create a résumé if you are solely interested in DIII? I think the investment of time is worthwhile for two reasons: one, if you are the only one submitting a résumé to a coach, you will stand out, and two, you are going to need one later in life for your professional career.

Players Who Created a Résumé	DI	DII	DIII
Percentage	79%	70%	58%

Here is an example of a résumé:

Cindy Soccer

csoccer@PigtailsToPreseason.com
1313 Super Soccer Lane
Madison, WI 53797
555.221.9696 (home)
555.222.9797 (cell)

Education

2002-2006   Edgewood High School, 1515 Monroe Street, Madison, WI 53533

Academic Achievement

Anticipated GPA 3.883   ACT 25
Current   GPA 3.872   SAT 1050   AP credits 10

Soccer Achievement

Awards   2003-present   All-City, All Conference
               2002   All City

High School   2002-present   Varsity Team
ODP   2001-present   State Team
Club   1999-present   Madison 56ers

Position   Forward
Stature   5'9", 155lbs
Statistics   2002-present   42 Goals, 35 Assists

Extracurricular Activities

2002-present   Ronald McDonald House—Volunteer
2002-present   Athletes against Drunk Driving—Treasurer
2002-2004   Edgewood Basketball Team—Varsity team member 2004
                 Hand bells choir member
2003   Spanish Club member

Interests

Reading
Playing the piano
Golf

References

Mrs. Pat Rengal   High School Coach   555.233.5761
Mr. Mike Smith   Club Coach   555.231.9823
Ms. Sue Peterson   ODP Coach   555.414.3981

Videotape

The videotape can be a very useful recruiting tool. Done correctly, the videotape can generate interest in you and encourage coaches to come see you play.

If you send your videotape to prospective coaches along with your initial cover letter and résumé and you are contacted by the coach or the assistant coach, that is a sign they are interested in recruiting you. Most coaches will either call or e-mail you when they plan to attend one of your games.

The videotape can help the coach establish his or her list of players to visit. This is especially true for coaches at a great distance. If a coach is unable to see you play a club, high school, or tournament game, the videotape may encourage him or her to send a trusted source who lives in the area to watch your game.

The most important item to consider when making a videotape is quality. I surveyed college coaches about the usefulness of videotapes and they all said that good quality is essential. When I asked about length, the consensus was a five-minute segment with short clips showing highlights, as well as movement on and off the ball.

The composition of the videotape should include a brief introduction, four minutes of footage, and close with your contact information. To make a five-minute tape may mean choosing from an entire season's worth of games. Be prepared to edit!

Interesting Data

I asked players within each division if they created a videotape, and the numbers were pretty small, with the lowest in DI. I was pretty surprised that more players didn't take the opportunity to create a video.

I can think of a few reasons why players may not have created a videotape: one, it takes a reasonable amount of effort and time to create a good video; two, if they were interested in programs close to home, they knew they wouldn't have any problems getting in front of the coach; and three, they may not have thought about a video or believed they didn't really need one.

Created a Video	DI	DII	DIII
Percentage	27%	39%	37%

If you decide to create a videotape, the following information may prove helpful in the process.

Introduction

- Introduce yourself.
- State the positions you play.
- State your number.
- Give a brief acknowledgment for watching the videotape.

Footage

- Showcase individual skill
- Movement on-and off-the ball
- Highlights
- Best competition
- Vision
- Speed of play
- Playmaking ability

Homemade Versus Professional

If you decide to use a professional videographer, unless they are very familiar with soccer, you may need to determine what footage is appropriate for the videotape and what is not. Keep in mind what college coaches have told me, whether you hire someone to film games for you or you film yourself, the videotape must be quality. As you begin to review footage, think about these things regarding the quality of the film:

- Close to the field
- Proper lighting
- Clear, not fuzzy
- Minimal background noise
- Clips organized by individual play, movement on-and-off-the-ball, shooting, etc.
- If you're highlighting field play, a circle can be placed around you on the film to identify your location.

Timeline

The videotape should be ready to send to coaches in the spring semester of your junior year. Thus, filming should begin the summer after your sophomore year and finish up in the fall of your junior year. Editing takes time, so leave yourself a few months for that, too.

Phone Calls

Throughout the recruiting process, you will communicate verbally with many of the coaches who are recruiting you. Thus, it is important to be prepared for the conversation so you sound interested, thoughtful, and professional.

Prior to July 1 of your junior year, coaches are not allowed to contact you. This does not mean you cannot contact them. On the contrary, you may call them with questions at any time. Make sure you are not calling just to be calling; make it a legitimate reason. Never call a coach and ask a question you previously asked. Maintaining a log book with phone conversations will keep you from making this mistake.

After July 1 of your junior year, coaches may begin to contact you. When coaches do begin calling you, they want to get to know you. Be prepared to talk about your academic goals, friends, interests, and soccer. Coaches are also pretty predictable; they usually call the same day and time each week. Have a notebook by the phone, go into a quiet room, and always be ready to ask them questions.

⚽ *To the Parent of a Future Collegiate Player*

This is where your daughter may really need your help. Communicating with coaches can be intimidating; encourage your daughter to be herself. Perhaps role play a couple of conversations until she gets the hang of it. Also, with regard to the cover letter and résumé, try not to edit them yourself. Make comments and suggestions in the margins and let your daughter make the changes. This will allow her to develop her own writing style and feel confident that it is her work, not yours.

 ## *To the Future Collegiate Player*

Writing a cover letter and résumé is not easy. However, once you get them done, they can open doors for you. They have the ability to convey a great deal of information about you, your academic and athletic abilities, and your interests. Take your time, make them something you are proud to send to prospective coaches, and don't be afraid to have everyone you know read them and give you feedback.

Researching Soccer Programs, Attending Official Visits, and Negotiating the Scholarship

The Goal Is in Sight!

> Research your options and use your official visits. The best way to decide on a university is to go there and see what they have to offer. Any coach can tell you anything on the phone, but being there is a completely different experience.
>
> *Jayme Butts, Forward,*
> *University of Arkansas-Little Rock*

Introduction

This chapter is about challenging the final defender in front of the goal to make the shot. It is really what you have been preparing to do since you started reading this book: identify soccer programs of interest, visit their campuses, and have the head coach offer you a position and money to play!

Sometimes, with the goal in sight, a bit of performance anxiety may creep into your psyche. It's like when there is a wide-open goal and you take the shot and it goes completely wide. No one can figure out how you missed it! I understand this feeling, and I am going to give you the tools to focus on the back of the goal to make sure the shot goes *left corner net*. By the end of this chapter you will be able to take on everything in your way with grace and finesse.

In this chapter you will use the research skills you learned in the chapter on "Divisions I, II, and III: Three Levels, Three Lifestyles," to refine your search to soccer programs that complement your goals. I will give you suggestions for organizing the research process and creating an attribute list (used to market yourself when coaches call you), a list of questions to ask coaches when they call each week and on your official visits, and questions to ask the players. At the end of the chapter are examples of conversation and scholarship trackers that will help you recall what you talked about each week with the coach and what he or she offered you to play.

You will also learn how many official/unofficial visits are allowed by the NCAA, what to expect, how to act, and who pays. I have collected data from players that detail the activities they encountered during their official visits, the money paid for travel and meals, and when offers to play were extended. This information is separated out by the three divisions.

Finally, you will learn about the negotiation process. The mantra I have used throughout the book, "It's not personal, it's business," will be repeated, as this is the time when you may find yourself taking things too personally. Data will be presented on the number of players who received scholarships and when they received their first offer to play: before, during, or after the official visit.

Researching Soccer Programs

As you begin to refine your research on soccer programs, the same resources you used in the chapter titled "The High School Years: What Really Matters: Grades!" will give you the additional information you now need.

- Check the university or college website. In addition to getting information on academics, climate, culture, setting (i.e., rural or urban), size, and majors, you will find information on their soccer program statistics, records, players, and names and addresses of coaching staff. If you read past articles, you may get a feeling for what the coaching staff values in a player and the style of play.

- The best soccer magazine I have seen is *Soccer America,* offered in hardcopy or online. *Soccer America* provides information about college and university soccer programs. It provides a listing of how many scholarships are available, names of coaches, addresses, soccer ranking, history of program, etc.

What to Research

Here is the type of soccer information you need to research:

- How many seniors have been on the team for the past three years? This is valuable information because you will know how many players and what positions the coach is recruiting. It may also be important information to know because if there are not many true seniors or red shirt seniors, the girls that have left the program may have left because they were unhappy. This is information that your happiness may depend on!

- When you visit the school, you can ask the players and the coach about the players who left the team. You can even contact the players themselves. Remember, the more you find out about the team and the coach, the better your chances are of making a well-informed decision.

- How long has the coach been with the program? If coaches are looking to advance their career, they may only stay with the team for approximately five years. If they have not been with the team very long, check out their previous coaching experiences and how long they were with each team.

- How many freshmen played or started on the team over the last few years?

- Style of play: if you are a possession player and the team is a kick-and-run team, your style of play may not match the team's. This could hamper your playing time.

Filing System

Create a filing system to manage letters of interest from coaches and information about the school. The goal of getting yourself organized is to not go into information overload and meltdown. This is an overwhelming process, especially if you are considering a lot of schools and trying to manage all the papers coming in.

Additionally, buy a thin notebook and title it *Questions to Ask the Coach*; you don't want to keep asking the same questions over and over again. Make sure you leave some space between each question to record the coach's responses. Look for the example at the end of the chapter.

Buy another thin notebook and title it *Scholarship Offers*. You want to be able to document each offer and which attribute you shared with the coach. Also look for this example at the end of the chapter.

Attribute List

At a moment's notice you may need to talk about your positive attributes to a coach. This can be a hard thing to do if you are not used to talking yourself up. Make a list of what you can contribute to each team and keep it readily available for when a coach calls. Most of your attributes will overlap for each team, but make sure there are a couple of things that are specific to each team.

When a coach calls, you should be ready to read two or three attributes off your list. After your phone conversation, be sure to document the attributes you talked about in your notebook.

Using a list of attributes provides the coach with important information about you and reminds him or her why you are worth recruiting and worth the additional money.

The Official Campus Visit

> First of all, you need to visit all the potential
> colleges you are considering. During your visit,
> you need to be aware of the gut feelings that are
> nagging at your heart. While you are on your
> visit, write down things you like and dislike
> about the school. Once you are home, compare
> the lists to the other schools. It is a process of
> elimination.
>
> *Amanda Faulknham, Forward,*
> *University of South Carolina–Aiken*

The campus visit can be a pretty exciting and scary event
all rolled up into one overwhelming package. With each
visit comes the excitement of finding *your* new school mixed
with feelings of being a small fish in a very large and unfa-
miliar pond.

As a rising senior in your high school, you know the lay
of the land, who's who, and what's what. Your high school
is familiar, homey, and predictable. College campuses are
usually larger than high school, with many being massive,
impersonal, and full of the unusual and unexpected.

So how do you accomplish all you need to do at a campus visit with these scary, overwhelming, and exciting feelings you are having all at once? Preparation. Prepare for
each visit like you are preparing for a test: devote time to
learning about the school and the soccer program, don't be
lured into choosing a program before you have considered
all the alternatives, and do your homework.

Remember, this is about finding a good fit for you. You
need to go into it with your eyes wide open. No program is
perfect, but if you understand its shortcomings going into

it, you will be much happier. Finding out a program wasn't what you expected is far worse than going into it knowing its faults and choosing to accept it *as is*.

NCAA Rules

Before you go on an official visit, you need to be aware of the NCAA rules for Divisions I and II. You may only attend five *official* (paid) campus visits. However, there are no rules regarding how often and how many *unofficial* (not paid) visits you may attend (barring your parents' financial solvency). For Division III, you may attend an unlimited number of *official* visits. You are eligible to attend official visits once you achieve senior status and can only receive one *official* visit per school.

Prior to any official visit, you must, according to the 2005–2006 NCAA Recruiting Guide, submit "a high school academic transcript and a score from the PSAT, SAT, PLAN, or an ACT test taken on a national testing date under national testing conditions."

There are tons of NCAA rules regarding the official visit, including length of stay, lodging, meals, and transportation. There are also requirements that govern the entire recruiting process and communication with players and coaches. You can access these online at NCAA.org.

Official/Unofficial Visits Notebook of Questions

The official/unofficial visits notebook is an easy way of managing and organizing your visits. Use it to keep track of the information you learn about each program. Divide the notebook into two sections: *Questions to Ask the Coach* and *Questions to Ask the Players*. Also, after each visit, be sure to immediately write down your impressions of the team, the coach, the college or university, and your gut feelings.

When you get down to final negotiations with the coach, you can look back on your initial feelings and thoughts about the school and soccer program to help you make a decision. I have started a list of questions to ask the coach and players. Please add more as you think of them.

Questions to ask coaches:

- Do you typically play/start freshmen? (You should already know the answer to this question based on your prior research. By asking it now, you are assessing the coach's honesty).

- If players have left the team before their senior year, ask the coach for an explanation. You should also ask the team this question and even contact the player or players who have left. Remember, you want to make a well-informed decision, and this information is important.

- Know the type of soccer each program plays. If you don't play that type, ask the coach why she or he is interested in you and how she or he sees your style complementing the team's or if the coach intends to change you.

- Ask what position the coach sees you playing. Again, you should already know what positions the coach needs filled.

- What is the coach's policy on scholarships after injury? For career-ending injury?

- Are fifth-year scholarships available?
- Has the coach ever decreased a player's scholarship?
- Are players evaluated each year for scholarship increases?
- What amount of time each week is committed to soccer when the team is in season? What about during off-season? What about spring season?

Questions to ask team members:

- Does the coach have/play favorites?
- Is hard work rewarded?
- Is the coach able to provide players with honest feedback regarding playing time, ability to contribute, etc.?
- Do most players get along on and off the field? (Do they hang out together after practice?)
- Does the team do much team building?
- What is the coach's interaction style? Yelling? Quiet? Degrading? Positive?
- If players have left the team before their senior year, ask their former team members why.

What to Expect

The official visit is used as a recruiting tool by coaches. An invitation for an official visit is your clue they probably plan to make you an offer to play in their program. The coach's goal is to get you to commit as soon as possible and for as little money as possible. Your goal, however, is to glean all the information you can from the official and unofficial visits, weigh all your options, and make a well-informed decision based on a set of criteria you have determined to be important for you personally, academically, and athletically.

The official visit, along with phone calls from coaches, can be very high pressure. Do not commit until you are ready. Do not succumb to the pressures. Here is what one player said about the pressure she experienced:

> I regret not taking all five of my visits. I was pressured into deciding on the money offer within a certain amount of days, so I jumped on that instead of doing a complete comparison of the other four schools I had scheduled visits for.
>
> *Jacquilyn Lacek, Forward/Midfield,*
> *Central Michigan University*

Here is another excellent piece of advice from a player:

> Be careful because coaches can occasionally be fake; you think they are one way because of a visit and then you get there and they are completely different. So make sure you find out from the players their opinions. Also, see how many players consistently leave the team and why, because my choice of school wasn't right for me. Last year a ton of people quit and even more will this year.
>
> *Anonymous,*
> *University of Houston*

As this player states, find out why players have left the team. This piece of information is data you need in order to make a well-informed decision. Remember to ask players you are not staying with! The players you stay with have been handpicked by the coach. Their perception of the coach, the team, the program, or the university may be somewhat skewed.

I asked players, "What did you do while on your official/unofficial visits?" and the data are listed in the chart below. Activities they participated in are broken down by each of the three divisions. I thought it was interesting that not every player has dinner with the coach. I would have thought coaches would want to have some quality one-on-one time with each of the players they were recruiting.

In reviewing the data, most players can expect to have dinner with the players across all divisions, as well as attend a soccer game. For DI, count on attending a party.

Activities	DI	DII	DIII
Dinner with coach	65%	32%	40%
Dinner with players	85%	64%	64%
Attend a soccer game	65%	41%	44%
Attend another sporting event	55%	29%	40%
Attend a party	78%	39%	47%

The other piece of information I want to mention in this section is that you should plan to stay in the dorms with the players. This offer will be extended to you prior to your visit by the coach. This is a great way to get to know the players, get a feel for the university, and then talk to the players, informally, about the program, the school, the coach, etc.

How to Act

The coach will be on his or her best behavior, highlighting stellar communication skills, a warm and friendly demeanor, the program's superb facilities, and the university's brightest spots. So, how should you act? The same! Be on your best behavior, show respect and appreciation for the money and time they have spent on you, and demonstrate your very best manners.

Given that 78% of the players in DI and almost 50% of players in DIII went to parties on their visits, this is the time to talk about what *not* to do during your official/unofficial visits. Don't taint the coach's or players' impressions of you by participating in *all* the party activities. Yes, go to the party, see what the players are like and what the campus is like, but do not partake of any alcoholic beverages! For the most important reason, you are underage! For the second reason, you are being judged on your behavior by the players taking you out. Resist this temptation because it will most likely be there.

The goal of the official visit is for the coach to sell you on the program, the school, the players, and the university, and ultimately to get you to commit to the program for as little money as possible. Your goal is to find a program that meets all your needs and to negotiate your best financial deal.

With these two opposing goals, the coach may ask very direct questions like, "How do you like the university?" hoping to lead you toward a commitment to the program. A normal response would be, "I like the university a lot." But beware of "I" statements because they can lead you toward a commitment before you are ready. Try to craft a response that does not begin with "I." In response to their question, you could say, "The university seems very nice and appears to have a lot to offer." Here are some additional examples:

186

Instead of: "I like the campus," try "The campus looks fun."
Instead of: "I can see myself playing here," try "The facilities are all well-kept."
Instead of: "I really like all the players," try "The players seem very nice."

Once the official visit is close to an end, be sure to thank the coach for her or his time and efforts. Tell the coach you enjoyed your visit and getting to know her or him, the players, and the university. Leave upbeat and noncommittal. Because it's all very exciting while you are there, you may feel kind of euphoric and want to blurt out that this is the school for you. Resist this feeling. Your head needs to be clear and your emotions rational when you make your decision.

Hopefully you have been taking notes while on your visit. If not, now is the time. On your way home, jot down your thoughts. Once you are home, compare the school against other schools you are considering.

Who Pays

When it comes to money, things can feel a little messy and awkward. Here is where you want to take the coach's lead and listen to what he or she is telling you. The coach will usually say something like, "I would like to take you to dinner/lunch/breakfast." That means they intend to pay. As for the travel expenses, I think it's perfectly okay to ask for gas money if you are driving or airfare if you are farther away and intend to fly. Don't be afraid to ask for the entire fare; you may get a portion or all of it paid for.

I have heard stories from girls about the university's plane coming and picking them up. Those stories occurred at programs where the school's football team had its own plane and generated a great deal of money. I really wouldn't expect that. But in reviewing the data, if you are interested in DI, it looks like 70% of the players who responded to my survey had some portion of their travel paid for.

To help you through the uncomfortable area of finances, I asked players, "What was paid for when you went on an official visit?" As the chart indicates, DI pretty much picks up most of the tab; for DII and DIII, most food is included in the visit. As a backup, always have some money on hand in case an offer to pay is not extended.

Expenses Paid	DI	DII	DIII
Travel (a portion)	70%	28%	17%
Breakfast	87%	52%	53%
Lunch	97%	78%	89%
Dinner	88%	68%	62%

When an Offer Was Extended

There is so much to think and worry about while on your official visit. However, there appears to be one thing you don't have to worry too much about, and that is having an offer to play made while on campus.

I asked players when they received an offer to play, and none had an offer extended during the official visit. Now, some had offers made *prior* to the visit, but not during. It would appear that for all three divisions, one week after the official visit is when most offers to play are extended. According to the players I surveyed in DIII, some attended a tryout where an offer was extended at the conclusion of the tryout.

Received Offer to Play	DI	DII	DIII
Before official visit	21%	0%	6%
During official visit	0%	0%	0%
During tryout	0%	0%	14%
1 week after visit	30%	53%	33%
2 weeks after visit	10%	13%	20%
3 weeks after visit	16%	28%	0%
More than 3 weeks after visit	23%	6%	27%

I also asked players how many programs pursued them aggressively, meaning more than just sending them materials about their program and school, but calling them, asking them for official visits, and/or offering them a scholarship. The data indicates that four to six programs aggressively pursued DI players, and one to three programs aggressively pursued DII and DIII players. The data are presented below:

Number of Programs Pursuing a Player	DI	DII	DIII
1-3	27%	43%	70%
4-6	47%	35%	23%
7-9	10%	4%	6%

* Some players did not respond to this question.

Negotiating the Scholarship

By this point you should know whether it's financially feasible to attend each school you are in contact with. You should also know if you qualify for any academic or need-based scholarships, ROTC, grants, or loans. This information will be solicited by the coach, but remember, this is business, not personal; you don't have to disclose this yet. If the coach knows you are receiving other monies, academic or need-based, he or she will offer you less. When asked, politely say: "I don't know if I'm going to qualify."

Also, depending on the coach, you or your parents may negotiate the scholarship with the coach. You need to be prepared if the coach only wants to deal with you and not your parents. If it's you the coach chooses to negotiate with, your parents will play an integral part in helping you process and prepare for each week's offer.

When Holly was going through the recruiting process, my husband, Michael, purchased a book on how to negotiate the scholarship. Shortly after he finished the book, we attended a game of one of the coaches who was recruiting her. After the game, during a conversation with the coach, the coach turned her back on us, faced Holly, and made her first financial offer.

Wow, we were pretty blown away that she turned her back on us. It was at this moment we knew Holly was going to have to negotiate her own scholarship with this coach. The coach clearly didn't want to deal with us.

As we left the field to go home, I remember Holly being angry at the offer. This is where Michael began to educate her on the process. This was merely the first of many offers. So the dance began...

Offers and Negotiations

Talking about money is never easy. Talking about how much you are worth is even harder. Combine this with the differing goals between you and the coach, and feelings can become hurt when the coach's scholarship offer doesn't match what you believe you are worth. If/when this occurs, remember the mantra:

It is not personal, it is business!

Since this is a business, you will need to do research regarding the school, the soccer program, and your family's financial situation. You want to enter into negotiations as well-informed as your adversary, the coach. To make your very best deal, you have to know most of what the coach knows in addition to some financial information about your family.

I have generated a list of questions below that you will need to get answered. I have divided them into *school/soccer* and *family/personal*. Once you have answered them to the best of your ability, place them in your file for that school for a quick reference.

School/Soccer

- How much scholarship money does the program have?
- How is the money distributed between players? Do some players receive full scholarships and others receive just enough for books or none at all?

- How many seniors are leaving and how much did they receive?
- How many players are currently on scholarship?

Family/Personal

- How much can your family afford to pay?
- Are you eligible for financial aid?
- Are you eligible for any academic scholarships?
- Are your ACT/SAT scores high enough to generate a merit scholarship?
- Are you interested in ROTC?
- What is the amount you are looking for?

Entertaining Multiple Offers

Just like during the recruiting process where you communicated with multiple coaches, during the negotiation process, you may find yourself negotiating with more than one coach. Negotiating with multiple coaches is perfectly acceptable. In fact, coaches are negotiating with more than one player at a time!

You do not want to miss out on getting the most money possible by only entertaining one coach's offer at a time. If you delay negotiating with a coach, he or she may move on to the next player he or she is interested in. If you come back later in the process hoping to begin negotiations because the first school did not work out, the amount of money on the table will probably have decreased.

Entertaining multiple offers simultaneously also helps you compare scholarships between schools. Reviewing multiple offers can also give you insight into your soccer value.

Things to Remember during the Negotiation Process:

- Never accept the first offer.

- The offers will increase each week.

- It's not personal, it's business. It's your job to get as much as you can; it's the coach's job to get you for as little as possible.

- Be prepared to explain your worth and talk yourself up (i.e., what you can contribute to the team).

- There will be a time when the coach says it is his or her final offer. Take it if this is the school and soccer program you want.

- Unless you are the next Mia Hamm, do not expect to receive a full scholarship.

The final question I asked players was, "Did you receive an athletic scholarship?" and the data were overwhelming for DI and DII. The majority of players within these two divisions received an athletic scholarship. DIII does not give athletic-based scholarships; I'm assuming the 28% of players who responded to my survey received either an academic or need-based scholarship.

Scholarship Received	DI	DII	DIII
Percentage	93%	95%	28%

⚽ *To the Parent of a Future Collegiate Player*

You have played an instrumental role in your daughter's soccer happiness as she has grown and developed into the young woman she is today. You have provided her with opportunities to play on good teams, given up your weekends to take her to tournaments, paid for camps and out-of-town travel, uniforms, new cleats every season, speed coaches, and everything in between.

In this chapter you have learned how to help your daughter find a soccer program that complements her soccer goals, you have assisted her with navigating official and unofficial visits, and finally, you have supported her through the negotiation process. These final tasks represent your love, your commitment, and your devotion to your daughter and her dream. These final tasks also represent an end. There is nothing more for you to do except provide her with opportunities to share her feelings and thoughts so she can begin to process all the information from her head and heart.

Questions to Ask the Coach

Name of coach:____

School:____

Date of conversation:___________

    Question 1____

      Answer 1____

    Question 2____

      Answer 2____

Date of conversation:___________

    Question 1____

      Answer 1____

    Question 2____

      Answer 2____

Date of conversation:___________

    Question 1____

      Answer 1____

    Question 2____

      Answer 2____

Scholarship Offers

Name of coach:_______________________________________

School:____

Date:________________

Offer:____

What you can contribute (list two or three things):

____

____

Date:________________

Offer:____

What you can contribute (list two or three things):

____

____

Date:________________

Offer:____

What you can contribute (list two or three things):

____

____

Date:________________

Offer:____

What you can contribute (list two or three things):

____

____

____

Choosing the Right School and Team

It's Like Falling in Love

> On my visit, it just felt like the place for me. Looking for a college is like falling in love: when it's the one for you, you can just feel it.
>
> *Amy Jackson, Defense,*
> *Northwest Missouri State*

Choosing a school and soccer program involves one of the most important decisions in your life, to date. In the chapter "Divisions I, II, and III: Three Levels, Three Lifestyles," I said that all good decisions involve both objective (the data) and subjective (your heart) considerations. Now is the time to talk about how your heart feels. Your happiness depends on it!

If you have done your research and know what type of soccer program and academic institution is best for you, and your heart is in total agreement, then you are set. Now you can begin to wade through the myriad of programs and schools in search of the perfect match.

But what if intellectually you have made a decision on a collegiate division or program but your heart feels a different way? What if you know, deep in your heart, that you must attend a particular school or program that is completely opposite of what you have determined is important for you academically, socially, and/or athletically? Listen!

Your heart won't be content until you give it a voice. Listen and then begin to gather more information. Do more research, take more official visits (if you have any left), or take as many unofficial visits as you need, and then continue to listen and learn until there is agreement between your head and your heart. Don't sign with any program until there is agreement. You have plenty of time to resolve the conflict. Don't be rushed.

Wherever you are along the continuum of making a decision, the players I surveyed have some advice for you to consider prior to making your decision final. They have been where you are today; they have felt the same anguish that comes with wanting to make the right decision and the same excitement that comes with knowing one's collegiate soccer career is around the corner.

I asked the collegiate players one final question: "What advice would you give a female in high school about picking a school?" I hope you find peace of mind in their advice.

> I would encourage her to ask questions, especially to the players, because I did not ask questions and when I got to school my first year during preseason, we were having three practices a day, each practice lasting two hours. I would also encourage her to ask questions about academic requirements, because as a freshman I had to attend mandatory study hall. I would also ask how the team gets along and views the coach. The most important thing is to make a decision that will make you happy, but also keep in mind

that it is not the end of the world if you do not like the choice of school you attended. You can always change.

Jen Mascarin, Forward,
University of South Carolina-Aiken

Do not—*do not*—just base your decision on soccer. There are many factors that play into your college experience. Many high school students think that soccer is going to be their career when in reality it will be done sooner than you think.

Rebecca Callen, Midfield/Defense,
Bloomsburg University

Take as many unofficial visits as you can to get a feel for the distance away from home you feel comfortable with, meet the coach, and ask questions! As far as your final decision, after your official visit, you should feel like you are at home. If you get that feeling where the team is like your sisters and you can stand being that far from home, then you are where you want to be for the next four years.

Becky Imhoff, Forward/Midfield,
University of Cincinnati

Talk to players without the coach around to get the inside scoop. Coaches are a lot different when they are your coach than they are when they want to be your coach.

Jenna Kickpatrick, Midfield/Defense,
Murray State University

Go somewhere that you feel comfortable with the team and with the area. Go to a school that has your major, because soccer is not the only reason you go to college. You attend college for an education. Trust me, when you visit colleges, you will know your school because you will fall in love. It will be the best years of your life! Have fun. Good luck!

Melissa Penney, Forward,
East Carolina University

Write a list of pros and cons, talk to current players, and don't forget about the academics.

Anonymous,
Providence College

Go with your gut reaction. If it seems like something is off on the team, there usually is. If players seem like they are putting up a front, they probably are.

Leah Glines,
Southwest Missouri State

First, you need to decide what you are looking for in a school: size, location, etc. Then you have to go with your instinct on how you feel when you visit the school. You will usually be able to tell right away if you would like the school, the community, and the people. And equally important is the soccer team and coaching staff. These are the people you will be spending the majority of your time with during your college career. Make sure they are people you will enjoy being around all the time! Also, make sure the coaches have plans for using you and that you are happy with their plan. You don't want to go to a school where they don't plan on using you your freshman year if all you want to do is play.

Melissa Robinson, Defense,
Western Kentucky University

Make sure you have asked every question you could possibly ask. Things are not always what they appear to be, so make sure you find out things about the team that you think you should know. Make sure you pick a school that has your major and where you feel you fit. And consider playing time and whether you think you can come in and contribute right away. When you find your school, you will just know it because it feels right.

Tenesha Duncan, Forward,
University of Oklahoma

Take your official visits. You may be unhappy if you don't see what a real weekend is like. Don't make decisions based on money alone. Also, get your name out there. Know the rules about recruiting, so if a coach doesn't call you, you will know whether it's because they are not interested or because the rules only allow them to call once a week.

Jennifer Walters, Defense,
Auburn University

First and most importantly, pick the school that is best for the career you will be pursuing. Know what type of school works best for you—small or big. Then, give yourself a chance to talk with players on the team that have different roles in order to get a real perspective of how things are.

Anonymous,
Michigan State University

Go with your heart; don't go just because the coach says that you're going to be an all-star or because they say your scholarship will increase each year, because coaches are telling everyone that. Go where you really want to go, and remember, the decision should not solely be based on soccer; education is what is going to be left when the glorious college years are over.

Kelly Wilmouth, Defense,
Texas A&M University

I would tell her to make sure she goes on her official visits and goes out with the girls. Don't just sit in the dorm rooms. Go out and meet other athletes. Also, don't settle for money; make sure you really like the college.

Vandi Odgen, Midfield,
Ball State University

Take your time! This could possibly be one of the most important decisions in your lifetime. Consider *all* aspects, not just the scholarship offer or the program availability. Consider distance, the team in general, your love for the game, and what you are hoping to achieve after your schooling.

Jodi Kulinitch, Forward,
University of South Carolina-Aiken

Use all your official visits and remember that education comes first. Make sure that the university has the major you want to study and a backup as well. Also, it is important to know what kind of classroom you learn best in.

Amanda Garcia, Midfield,
Clemson University

Pick a school based on academics first. After your college years are over, you're going to need a degree to fall back on. Soccer is not life and it definitely cannot support you through the rest of your life. (It took me my whole college career to discover this.) Next, make sure you pick a team that your personality gels with. Your team will be your new family for the next four years, so it's important you like and get along with them.

Anonymous,
Penn State University

You've heard it a million times: don't pick a school solely on a coach or your opportunity to play on a team. Be aware that you take a risk when you base your decision on athletics. A number of things may happen: the coach might leave, as occurred with my track coach, who retired in the middle of the year; you may find yourself injured and unable to participate for a year; the playing time you expected may not be what you actually receive (an experience shared by many); you may find that your classes require more time than you can give them while playing varsity sports and that the time commitment for practices, travel, team activities, etc. is more than you expected. I have a number of friends who chose to attend school for athletic reasons who discovered that, although they loved their chosen sport, upon experiencing college, they did not want to commit so much time and effort at the level required in collegiate athletics.

Kristen Werder, Forward,
Clarion University of Pennsylvania

Don't listen to anyone but yourself when picking a school. Seriously! You will be the one sitting in class, being in your room, being with your team, and being in the area you choose, not your mom or dad! You will find a school that will fit you perfectly, I promise. It may not be the week after July 1, but in due time it will come.

Anonymous,
West Virginia University

I felt I was supposed to play here when I came on my visit.

Chelsea Hipley, Forward/Midfield,
California State Polytechnic-Pomona

Make sure you are picking a school that has your field of study. Make sure you can see yourself there for four or more years (campus, coaches, team values, and teammates). Make sure you are dedicated and prepared enough to play soccer for another four years at a very high, demanding level.

Michelle Noble, Defense,
Central Michigan University

Make sure you know what you are getting yourself into. DI is awesome because of the conferences and competition and all the other aspects you get with it, but don't let that be the only thing you look for. Make sure you *love* the game and know that it takes a lot of commitment and hard work. It's not a cake walk.

Erin McDowell, Midfield,
Iowa State University

Take your time and do not rush. Almost every freshman I have talked to has considered quitting at one point or another in her freshman year. When you choose a school, make sure you feel it inside. Don't let anyone pick for you. Don't be influenced by where your high school or club coaches or your parents want you to go. Take their advice into consideration, but you are the one who makes the final decision because you have to go do the work at the program.

Jacquelyn Lacek, Forward/Midfield,
Central Michigan University

Go on recruiting trips and really ask yourself if you can see yourself going there. Do you like the town? Do you like the girls and coach? Keep in mind that how the coach is on your recruiting trip probably won't be the same during your season (meaning they'll be a lot nicer and usually tell you what you want to hear when recruiting). Consider what level or division it is and if you're willing to give that much of yourself. You have to remember that college soccer is like a job. It's extremely demanding. It is physically, mentally, and emotionally draining.

Katie Behrens, Forward/Midfield,
University of Tennessee-Martin

You have the entire country to pick from! This is your time to do what you want and live where you want. Pick a school where you will be happy. Weigh your options and figure out what is important to you. I have friends who got full rides to DII schools, but chose a DI school simply because they *had* to go DI. Start the research early; know all your options. Make sure you have a good GPA too; you don't want to limit yourself just because you have bad grades. Don't be afraid to ask the coaches tons of questions about the school and program.

Anonymous,
University of West Florida

Visit, visit, visit. If you are traveling for soccer or anything else, check ahead of time if there is a college in the area and visit it. Walk around, talk to students, check out the student union/center. I must have visited twenty-five schools in NC, SC, and VA. Check out schools on www.princetonreview.com. Talk to other college kids. Then start narrowing schools down by deciding if you would like to be close to home or far away, small or big, if they have your major, if you want a school near the beach or in the mountains, etc. Set big goals by applying to schools you would like to get into but may not. Then apply to ones that maybe aren't your first choice but you would still like to attend.

Kathleen Blake, Goalkeeper,
Catawba College

Start early. Look for schools you are interested in and contact their coaches. Show them what you are made of and prove to them you belong on their team! Pick a school that will make you happy and let you excel in your career. Go for the school with the best to offer you. College is about you. Pick a school that is going to make you happy and allow you to be comfortable. This will help you feel secure and at home at the school.

Jessica Corsey, Forward,
Barton College

Talk to other players on the soccer team. Ask them how the coach handles wins and losses. Does he/she ask how your day has been? Find out what the turnover rate is. If more players are leaving every year than just seniors, something is probably wrong. Yes, not everyone will stay, but if many players are leaving every year, then something is amiss. If possible, contact past players because they have nothing to lose by telling you anything negative. Most important of all, don't make your decision after talking to just one school. Go on as many visits as you can. Write notes after each visit. Write down what you like and do not like about the soccer program, coaching staff, and school. This way, visiting all schools, you will have your notes that you can look back on when reflecting.

Laura Crews, Forward,
Pfeiffer University

Don't pick a school because your friends are going there. Pick a school because it's what you like. College is about meeting new people and experiencing different things. If you continue college with all of your high school friends, then you are missing out on the entire experience. When you go out into the world and start working, you will have to meet new people and network. Staying in your comfort zone doesn't allow for growth or new opportunities.

Lairin King, Midfield/Defense,
Clayton College

Always remember that no matter where you choose, you can always go somewhere else if it is not a perfect fit.

Kristin Ramaglia, Defense,
California State Polytechnic-Pomona

⚽ To the Future Collegiate Player

I hope these quotes from the collegiate players help you gain knowledge from their experiences, wisdom about the decision-making process, and inspiration from their journey. I wish you the best!

I have enjoyed being a small part of your journey. Remember, there is no such thing as mistakes—only interesting twists and turns that guide you to your destiny. Embrace the unknown and your heart.

⚽ To the Parent of a Future Collegiate Player

As your daughter embarks on her new journey to college, she will experience many changes. Your role as she transitions from a young girl to a woman will change from advocate, biggest fan, keeper of the house rules, and academic sentinel to include being her friend. The most important thing you can do in this new role is always be there to listen to her.

Once your daughter makes a commitment to attend a soccer program, she will continue in soccer as a young adult. She will be required to uphold standards—academic, social, and athletic—set by her coach, the university, and the NCAA. You are to be celebrated for all that you have done. When she is older, she will understand the depth of your gift. As a fellow parent of two collegiate soccer players, I understand!

Glossary

"A" Pool

At ODP camp, some players are chosen from the state team for the "A" pool. "A" pool is the highest pool team at camp. These players are being considered for the next level, which is the regional pool team.

Academic Ineligibility

Rules in college set by the NCAA that set GPA cutoffs for academic eligibility. If you don't meet the minimum standard you will be "ineligible to play."

Academic major

An academic major is what you choose to study in college. It will be what you take the majority of your classes in. A few examples of academic majors are: physical education, engineering, aviation, and English literature.

Academic Requirements

Each college/university has academic requirements established for admissions and for continued study. The NCAA also has academic requirements for play.

Admissions Dean

Someone who collects all your credentials: academics, athletics, volunteerism, etc., and presents them at a committee meeting to determine eligibility, any unique contribution you make to the student body or school, and admission to the university or college.

Agility training

Activities and drills that develop speed and dexterity.

All City/All State

These are titles bestowed on a select few players in high school. They are determined by nomination by city and state coaches. These titles mean that within all of the city and within all of the state, the player is one of their top eleven.

Assistant coach

The assistant coach carries out the instructions of the head coach. His or her responsibilities vary depending on the needs of the head coach. If the assistant has a particular expertise, it may be used in practice (e.g., if he or she played goalie in college, then one of his or her responsibilities might be to work with the goalies).

"B" Pool

At ODP camp some players are chosen from the state team for the "B" pool. "B" pool is the second highest pool team at camp. These players show promise for the "A" pool.

Career-ending injury

Sometimes players are injured or re-injured to the point where they are unable to continue to play competitively. Their formal soccer career ends due to the injury.

Career Inventory

During high school, a career counselor will provide inventories for students to take to help determine career interests.

Competitive/Select/Premier Team

The focus of this type of team is on competition. Players must try out. Only the most skilled or talented players are invited to join. This team usually travels across the state for league play and attends tournaments within the state, region, and sometimes internationally.

Cooper Test

The aim of this test is to run as far as possible in exactly *twelve minutes*. The distance covered will then give a rough estimate of one's fitness. The test is only recommended for trained persons because it demands maximum effort. It is conducted around a soccer field.

DI, DII, DIII

There are three divisions of athletics in college: Division I, II, and III. Within these three divisions are three distinct levels of competition, commitment, and lifestyle for the athlete. The most rigorous and demanding of the levels is DI. Athletic scholarships may be given to players at DI and DII.

Event team

As a member of ODP, some players from the team are chosen to represent their state at an "event." Players usually have to tryout for the event team.

Exhibition games

Teams play other schools not in their conference during preseason.

Fartleks

Fartlek is Swedish for *speed play*. It's a combination of jogging, running, and sprinting, followed by a slow jog to recover. This sequence is repeated multiple times.

Field positioning (on/off the ball)

An understanding of where a player is supposed to be, at any moment during a game, given the position they play on the field and when they have the ball (on) or not (off the ball).

Fifteen Seconds of Fun

Players sprint ninety yards in fifteen seconds, jog back in forty-five seconds. This interval may be repeated from twelve to twenty times.

Fitness

One's level of physical condition.

GPA

Grade point average. This is a calculation based on number of credits earned and the grade points associated with them.

Guest coach

An invited coach from another club or college who is invited to speak, motivate, or train players.

Head coach

At the college level, the head coach is the person responsible for the team and its wins and losses. At some schools, the head coach's contract may be terminated if the team does not have a winning season.

Individuals

Coaches work with each athlete one-on-one to refine and develop each player's position and skills.

In season

The time when a college team plays other teams within its conference for the opportunity to play in the NCAA.

Kick and run

This type of play is characterized by kicking the ball somewhere on the field and another player running to get it. It is not a controlled style of soccer, and it is somewhat haphazard.

Lift

Weight training.

Mental toughness

Mental toughness is the ability to focus, to achieve, and to become all that is inside of you while dealing with self-doubt, criticism, and tough competition.

National Signing Day

February 1 is the first day you are eligible to sign a Letter of Intent to play soccer for a DI and DII school when an athletic scholarship is involved. There is no rush, though! You can sign later if you are not sure or are in the process of negotiations.

National team

The national team is the feeder team to the International Olympic team. It is the highest team in the Olympic Development Program.

NCAA Clearinghouse

DI and DII use the Clearinghouse to evaluate your academic eligibility. They review your core courses taken in high school, GPA, and standardized test scores from the ACT and SAT. For DIII, contact the colleges for specific policies and financial aid.

Networking

The skill of utilizing one's contacts, friends, friends of friends, friends of family, etc., to acquire something of personal value.

ODP

Olympic Development Program. Within most states there will be an Olympic Development Program that provides opportunities for players to compete for a spot in the program. ODP is organized by age and is highly competitive. There are eight levels of ODP: state pool team, state team, regional pool team, regional team, national pool team, national team, and the Olympic pool team and Olympic team. Each level exists to feed the next. Players are picked to advance to the next level at a regional camp held yearly.

ODP camp

Players who make the state, regional, or national team compete for the next level of play during ODP camp. Competition is fierce, the pressure is significant, and emotions run high.

Official visit

Players interested in DI and DII get five official visits to colleges/universities. An itinerary is established and a portion of all travel expenses and food is paid. DIII players may attend as many official visits as they wish.

Parent representative

A parent volunteer from the club team who manages the team finances, coordinates tournaments and team events, orders uniforms and bags, and works directly with the coach.

Playmaking ability

This is a player's aptitude to set up a play that may result in a positive outcome for the team, such as a goal.

Pool team

The pool team is comprised of players who have been selected to train together in order to pick the state, regional, or national team. In the world of soccer, being able to place "pool team" on your soccer résumé is a positive credential.

Possession play

This type of play is characterized by possessing the ball; it is a very controlled play with deliberate passes to players.

Preseason

The designated time prior to a team's competitive season. Preseason involves multiple trainings in a day, team bonding activities, and a lot of competition between players. This is the time when players are scrutinized for starting positions.

Recruiting process

For the junior/senior in high school, the methods a player may use to get recruited. It may involve identifying which schools to apply to, talking to coaches, creating a soccer résumé, creating a videotape, visiting colleges and soccer programs, and negotiating a scholarship.

Recreational team

The recreational team is usually the first type of team players are exposed to. The focus is on fun, introducing the young athlete to the sport, and recreation. The score may or may not be kept.

Red shirt player

Red shirt is a term used to signify a player who is not officially playing with the team for the season. Sometimes players red shirt due to an injury, and freshmen often red shirt to further develop their skills and abilities before beginning play for the team. If the player is under scholarship, it does not affect their scholarship eligibility.

Regional team (ODP)

The regional team is comprised of players who have been selected from the ODP state camp. They represent a region in the United States.

Regional traveling team (Club)

The regional traveling team is the highest level of league competition for a club team. Depending on your state, some regional team players may forgo their high school soccer team to join this team. These teams travel throughout the region for competition and often play college teams that are in their off-season.

ROTC

Reserve Officer Training Candidate. A program where scholarship money is awarded in exchange for military commitment.

SAT/ACT

College entrance exams used by colleges and universities for admissions. Most Eastern schools prefer the SAT, but most will accept the ACT.

Scholarships

There are opportunities to have a portion or all of one's tuition covered by scholarships. They can be awarded for athleticism, academics, based on need, or through a military commitment such as ROTC.

Scrimmage

When a team is divided at least twice and the smaller teams play each other for practice.

Skill/technical development

This is learning how to strike the ball properly, shoot, juggle, dribble, and do taps and various moves such as step-overs, scissors, etc.

Small-sided games

Games where there are fewer players on the field than usual. Normally there are eleven players on the field, but with small-sided games that number is fewer.

Soccer America

A magazine containing a list of all colleges/universities with soccer programs. This magazine lists contact information, number of scholarships, and other relevant information.

Soccer credentials

In the context of club coaches, soccer credentials are the licenses the coaches hold and their previous experiences, both playing and coaching. Each license indicates the level to which the coach has devoted training and holds particular knowledge.

Soccer politics

In soccer you just can't get away from the politics, whether it is contrived or real. The stories I have heard are like urban legends. Suffice it to say, soccer politics involves all the seediness of disgruntled people.

Speed of play

This is a player's ability to speed her play up or down depending on what is required to achieve a positive outcome for the team.

Spring season

The time when teams who aren't in each other's conference play each other to continue skill development.

State Cup tournament

Within each state a State Cup tournament is held. Any team is eligible to participate. Winning this tournament provides status of the best team in the state and an opportunity to advance to regionals and nationals.

State team (ODP)

The state team is comprised of players who have been selected from the state's pool team.

Tactical development

This is the ability of a player to anticipate where the ball will be placed by their opponent prior to its placement. It's a comprehensive understanding of the game during play and knowledge of how and when to attack.

Technical aptitude

This includes a player's ability to correctly execute foot skills, headers, drills, trapping, etc.

Trainers (Athletic)

At the college level, trainers are present for all practices and games in case of an injury. The trainer determines whether a player is released for play after an injury.

Trainer

People who are paid to come in and teach a particular skill or concept to a team. Many are brought to a practice to teach speed or agility training and tactical skill development.

U-8, U-14

The "U" stands for under. Thus, a U-8 team is comprised of players under eight years old. The U-14 team is comprised of players under fourteen years old. Just like the cut-off dates for kindergarten, there are cut-off dates for when your daughter turns a certain age that determine into which age division she is placed.

Unofficial visit

An unoffical college visit is one where the player initiates contact with the coach and/or school to set up a visit. The player pays for all of her own travel and food expenses.

Vision

This is a player's ability to "read" the entire field and anticipate plays and movement.

Warm-ups (clothes)

Competitive teams will usually have their team in matching sweats and jackets prior to games. It's a nice showing of solidarity and, in inclement weather, provides warmth for the muscles prior to play.

Winter season

The time when teams do not formally compete, but continue to develop their skill and tactical development.

World Cup

A soccer game taught in the younger years and usually played at the end of practices as a reward at the higher levels.

Endnotes

a   Ellison, Katherine. "You're Entitled." Women's Health Magazine, 2006, July/August Issue.

b   United States Olympic Committee. http://www.USOlympicTeam.com.